FRONTIER TERROR

MURDER, LYNCHING, AND VIGILANTES IN THE OLD WEST

MICHAEL RUTTER

TWODOT®

Essex, Connecticut
Helena, Montana

T0268111

To my wife, Shari Welsh-Rutter

A · TWODOT® · BOOK
An imprint of Globe Pequot, the trade division of
The Rowman & Littlefield Publishing Group, Inc.
4501 Forbes Blvd., Ste. 200
Lanham, MD 20706
www.rowman.com

Distributed by NATIONAL BOOK NETWORK

Copyright © 2023 by Michael Rutter

All rights reserved. No part of this book may be reproduced in any form or by any electronic or mechanical means, including information storage and retrieval systems, without written permission from the publisher, except by a reviewer who may quote passages in a review.

British Library Cataloguing in Publication Information available

Library of Congress Cataloging-in-Publication Data
Names: Rutter, Michael, 1953- author.
Title: Frontier terror : murder, lynching, and vigilantes in the Old West / Michael Rutter.
Other titles: Murder, lynching, and vigilantes in the Old West
Identifiers: LCCN 2022043669 (print) | LCCN 2022043670 (ebook) | ISBN
   9781493067725 (paperback) | ISBN 9781493067732 (ebook)
Subjects: LCSH: West (U.S.)—History—19th century. | Outlaws—West (U.S.)—History—19th
   century. | Frontier and pioneer life—West (U.S.)
Classification: LCC F593 .R88 2023 (print) | LCC F593 (ebook) | DDC
   978/.02—dc23/eng/20220920
LC record available at https://lccn.loc.gov/2022043669
LC ebook record available at https://lccn.loc.gov/2022043670

∞™ The paper used in this publication meets the minimum requirements of American National
Standard for Information Sciences—Permanence of Paper for Printed Library Materials, ANSI/
NISO Z39.48-1992.

CONTENTS

CONTENTS

INTRODUCTION

Frontier Terror isn't a feel-good book. It is not supposed to be. It is about real people who didn't make good choices—and those who lived and died in fear because of those choices. We have learned that it is important to ask hard questions, even if we know the answers may not be pleasant or fit into convenient cultural cubbyholes. The inconvenient truth is that some parts of our history are not pretty. Maybe they should give us nightmares. Perhaps we can learn from the past. It's important to inspect and question established historical orthodoxies to see if they are accurate or include alternative points of view. The intent is not to bust icons or belittle cherished tidbits of history. Recalibration keeps us centered as we learn to think in new ways. We cannot excuse or justify unprincipled actions.

The 1844 Regulator-Moderator War was one of the bloodiest feuds in the West, lasting four years. It would be good to report that frontier men and women learned valuable lessons during this bloodbath, but they did not. Rather, this feud set the tone for future range wars. Two important questions emerged: Who owned the land and how was the land to be used? Greedy men and bullies didn't appreciate discussion. They preferred violence and intimidation. Their arbitration was rope, gun, knife, and fire. The war became a series of retaliatory vendettas. The Johnson County War in Wyoming became so intense that large cattlemen hired a train-load of Texas gunslingers to kill the small ranchers. The Lincoln County War was a fight between cattle barons, but Billy the Kid was remembered the best from that conflict. Mostly, ranchers didn't take kindly to the government selling homesteads to squatters on open range they had used for years without anyone getting in their way. The Brown's Park Range War was different. In a remote corner of Utah and Colorado, a cattle baron named Orah Ben Haley decided he wanted a mountain valley called Brown's Park. In this war, the issue wasn't squatters. Haley wanted to steal established ranch lands because he thought he could.

The legendary Texas Rangers were touted as the nonpareil good guys in Western mythology. However, the Rangers don't survive a fact check. The popular opinion about the Rangers probably would not be shared by those of Mexican, African, or American Indian heritage in the nineteenth century. In addition to fighting outlaws, the Rangers were the state's instrument for ethnic cleansing. They enforced Jim Crow and Juan Crow policies. Latinos were especially fearful. The Rangers were sometimes referred to as the KKK of the Texas border.

Our history is a curious amalgamation of triumph and tragedy. Nephi Johnson and his Mormon parents traveled across the Midwest hoping to find religious freedom. They lost their homes to angry mobs of men and persecution. In Nauvoo, Illinois, Nephi saw the body of Joseph Smith, the Mormon Prophet, who had been murdered by a mob. He crossed the Plains in the Mormon migration and settled in southern Utah Territory. He was also a soldier in the Mormon militia. His church leaders had made bad moral choices resulting in the Mountain Meadows Massacre. They ordered the slaughter of 130 men, women, and children on a wagon train bound for California. Against his better judgment, Nephi obeyed orders and participated in what was nothing less than mass murder. This killing field has been described as a "perfect commotion" of gore. Later church leaders tried to cover their crimes by blaming the Paiute Indians. Like the other soldiers, Nephi had taken a vow of silence, a vow he could not keep. On his deathbed, his last words were, "The Blood. The Blood."

The twisted story of a scalp hunter named John Glanton is the opposite of Nephi Johnson's story. Glanton took pleasure in murder. He seems beyond redemption. We find him hard to fathom. He reminded his men to include the ears when they took a scalp because the Mexican officials who paid scalp bounties were less likely to haggle. He was hired to kill Apache Indians, but Navajo, Yuma, or Mexican scalps would do.

Forging a new country is hard work. The dross, however, must be measured in human terms. The quotient has a blast radius. In 1897, forty men rode to Williamsport, North Dakota, in the middle of the night. After tying their horses near the jail, they took three American Indians from their cell and hung them. They felt it was their duty. The Indigenous men would hang until the next evening when someone cut them down. In their opinion, the only good Indian was a dead one.

Bullet points on a timeline or snippets rarely move beyond cursory snapshots or stereotyped assumptions. Some threads are complex. An example would be the hanging of Black field hand Jesse Washington, who was mentally challenged. He was taken from a courtroom in Waco, Texas. Vigilantes put a chain around his neck, castrated him, and paraded him through the streets. The town cheered as the seventeen-year-old was lynched. He was raised and lowered over a bonfire in the town square. But there were other victims as well—the schoolchildren. Because it was the lunch hour, teachers led their classes to the town square for a civics lesson. Washington's scorched body was ostensibly an objective correlative about segregation.

The power of printed mediums—tabloids and newspapers—was also terrifying because it was used to manipulate public opinion and negotiate a different narrative. the *Cheyenne Sun* and the *Cheyenne Daily* were the most powerful newspapers in the Wyoming Territory in 1889. Two newspapermen, Ed Towse and Archie Slack, were responsible for a series of newspaper articles that misdirected history for almost one hundred years. These spin doctors vindicated and justified six murdering ranchers while they buried a woman named Ella Watson in a sea of slander. They rebranded her as a whore and rustler named Cattle Kate. Her crime? Filing a homestead on open range.

A sanitized history should be more frightening to us than the truth. Wilhelm Frick was tasked with rewriting history to justify the Third Reich. He argued it should not be objective because such notions were the fallacy of liberals. "The purpose of history was to teach" the doctrines of the state and Aryan supremacy.

Different perspectives give us the humility to understand why a person or a group of people behaved; it's not necessarily a nod of approbation. Histories from a single point of view do not tell a complete story. We need perspective and context to have a multidimensional understanding. The United States, warts and all, has been a brilliant social experiment. A study of our heritage is a journey and not a destination.

1

EAST TEXAS REGULATOR-MODERATOR WAR

THE BLOODIEST RANGE FEUD IN TEXAS HISTORY

I think it advisable to declare Shelby County . . . [a] free and independent governments and let them fight it out.

—Sam Houston

TEXAS, 1841–1845

Perhaps the devil went down to Georgia, but the settlers in the Sabine River Valley were certain Lucifer, himself, had staked a claim in Shelby County. In the Piney Woods of Deep East Texas, land troubles were brooding hot and ready to erupt. The war officially started on a calm day in April 1841, when Charles Jackson collected his Kentucky long rifle and saddled his mare. With his wife's blessing, he rode into Shelbyville, Texas, to kill Joseph Goodbread. It wasn't his first killing. Jackson lived by a code that demanded blood if his honor was questioned. He cocked his rifle as he rode up to the unarmed man. He told him to stand. Goodbread started to speak, but Jackson wasn't there to talk. He pulled the trigger and watched Goodbread die. Jackson's shot may not have been heard around the world, but it was heard in Texas. Mrs. Goodbread, mother and wife, had become the first official widow in what became the Regulator-Moderator War. In a few months, Mrs. Jackson would be a widow, too, and certainly not the last. Blood would flow freely in East Texas for the next four years.

The Regulator-Moderator War would prove to be the bloodiest vigilante action in Texas—and arguably in the history of the West—but it became more than a range war. It was, in reality, a civil war, and sadly, it foreshadowed a greater war that would soon divide the nation. It prefigured the murderous raids of Bloody Bill Anderson, the Quantrill's Raiders, and the Red Leg Jayhawkers. Under the pretense of establishing order, the blood feud began. It was a battle between rival factions—not unlike crime bosses or street gangs fighting turf wars. Each side was willing to carve out an unfair portion by force.

In this chapter, we will look at the influences that were factors in creating this four-year blood feud. It's tempting to point out the obvious as cause and effect: land speculation, fraudulent land claims, livestock rustling, and conflicts between new homesteaders and those who were established. But as we look more carefully, it's important to consider other persuasions that helped form such a malignant perfect storm. These include the confusion over land grants beginning in Mexican Texas and continuing after the Texas Revolution and the convolution of land acquisitions making the system an easy target for unscrupulous land agents and speculators. The chaos and displacement this caused for settlers was exacerbated by a weak central government, great distances, an unpredictable legal system, and the influences of local corruption. As the Texas historian Dr. C. L. Sonnichsen argues in *Ten Texas Feuds*, "the pattern laid out" in the Regulator-Moderator War became the prototype for the many that would follow.

FORMING THE MODERATORS AND REGULATORS

In Shelby County, the new settlers formed a vigilante "law-and-order" group called the Regulators. They wanted to "regulate" the action of the "lawless" older settlers who they considered land pirates and swindlers. They quickly went too far, taking the law into their hands and prospering their own business interests. To check the Regulators, a second vigilante group formed—again, in the name of law and order. They called themselves the Moderators. Their intention was to "moderate" the Regulators who had impacted their business interests. If this isn't confusing enough, later another group of vigilantes, called the Reformers, also a law-and-order group, entered the picture. And, as you've no doubt assumed, their intention was to reform.

It was good land, but it was a contested land . . . and had been for a long time. It had consistently been a dangerous place to make a living. Life was cheap, cattle rustling was a business practice, and real estate fraud was an art form. But, in a rough way, it had limply governed itself. It was hundreds of miles from official law and order, and with the new Texas Republic suffering from growing pains, it could not afford to send a stabilizing force.

Even under ideal conditions, real estate is a messy business because the devil is always in the details. There are invariably differing opinions that tie up courtrooms for years. Private and public land battles are reduced to who the legal owner is or how the land will be used. More specifically, someone had to answer the nagging questions of who the original owner was, if that person had the right to sell, or if there was some kind of agreed-on legal or quasi-legal due process or patent to the land transfer. Skim your newsfeed and you'll be inundated by current land and land-use issues, such as grazing and water rights; impact issues about fossil fuel versus renewable energy; tribal disputes about salmon runs and damming rivers; and logging and mining development and their effect on climate change, commercial fishing, wolves, or grizzly bears.

THE NEUTRAL GROUND

After the Louisiana Purchase, neither Spain nor the United States could agree on the border between Texas and Louisiana. To prevent conflicting over unsettled details, the two nations agreed to a neutral ground, sometimes called the Sabine Strip. The strip was from the Sabine River on the west to the Arroyo Hondo River on the east, and no settlements or developments would be permitted. Later, ownership went to the United States at the Adams-Onis Treaty in 1819. However, the neutral ground was not settled when Mexico gained its independence from Spain in 1821. This area became an ideal place for outlaws, enslavement, stolen livestock, and smuggling. It would soon become a problem for settlers in Shelby, Nacogdoches, San Augustine, and Harrison Counties.

GONE TO TEXAS

Mexico was eager to colonize Texas. Officials hoped such a move would develop the region's abundant natural resources and stimulate economic development. Additionally, controlled Mexican colonialization would ensure Mexico's borders against the growing United States. It would also help buffer existing settlements against the warring Kiowa and Comanche tribal nations. Colonial laws passed in the 1820s invited immigrants from the United States under the direction of an *empresario*, an official land agent. Stephen F. Austin is probably the most well-known. By late in the 1820s, Austin had settled twelve hundred immigrants on four million acres in Southeast Texas. It was his job as empresario to convince people to move to Texas and assist them in relocating. Naturally, Austin was also the liaison with Mexico and the governor of his settlements. For his participation, he received a large portion of land.

After the economic panic of 1819, colonization in Texas was an attractive option and not only for the adventurous but for struggling farmers, especially in the lower Mississippi Valley. As a bonus, Texas had no extradition laws, so those who'd lost farms or businesses and were facing debt collectors or debtor's prison could escape and begin again. It should be noted that Texas was also alluring to those pressed into indentured service or those wanted by the law. The famous phrase "gone to Texas" became a byword for hope or a "French leave," where someone packs up and disappears overnight. Gone to Texas on a piece of paper in a window or nailed to a door was enough said. It was Texas or bust. "If you're going to dream, dream big because everything is bigger in Texas." The promise of land was nearly unfathomable. Such folks were told the journey was dangerous and difficult—paved with graves and uncertainty—but it was land for the taking. Those were magic words. In the United States, land was selling for about $1.25 an acre, which meant about $100 for a farm; the entire sum was often required up front. In Texas, however, a settler was awarded a handsome headright. That was 4,605 acres of grazing land, or a league, and 177 acres of irrigatable land, referred to as a *labor*. The cost was $184, and it was not due for six years. A settler could own more acres than most of the fancy plantations. By 1830, there were more than 30,000 Americans in Texas. This was a sizable population when compared to other states or territories in the area (140,000 in Missouri; 215,700 in Louisiana; 136,00 in Mississippi; 30,038 in Arkansas Territory; and 34,700 in Florida Territory). The Mexican population in Texas was arguably around 6,000. Mexico was cash poor and trying to support itself, having nothing to enrich its coffers but land. There were abundant natural resources: Texas had more forest than California but little hard cash.

SHOOTING JOSEPH GOODBREAD

Joseph G. Goodbread and his group of con men were considered the "older settlers." He was a caring father to his seven children and kind and affectionate to his wife, but his business deals were shady, if not downright dishonest. His specialty was fraudulent land speculation and sales. Goodbread was more like a syndicate godfather than a member of the Better Business Bureau. He was a cunning opportunist who knew how to spin crooked deals and take advantage of the naivete and desperation of the new settlers. He was able to capitalize on the confusions of the Mexican land grant dispersions, especially after the uncertainties of the Texas Revolution. His crookery and underhanded dealings were perpetuated by his close associations with the equally slippery Shelby board of commissioners and other officials who helped by providing questionable land certificates. He was backed up by enforcers, tough men he'd hired from the Sabine Strip, men not afraid to use a gun or a rope. His men assisted him in some of his other ventures, rustling, smuggling, and enslaving. He had little patience for those who stood up to him. When "the newcomer," Charles Jackson, ran for office, Goodbread used his power to defeat Jackson. When Jackson set out writing letters to officials and newspapers, specifically calling Goodbread and his associates land pirates, he'd had enough. Goodbread sent Jackson a letter telling him stick to his affairs or be killed. The land pirate misjudged his reader.

Jackson was from Kentucky and was a likeable, mercurial man. He was tempered and carried a grudge if he felt he was being bullied or pushed; he was never one to back down. Dr. Levi Ashcroft, who knew him, said, he had "a reckless bearing," but he had "a rough eloquence" and made friends easily. He'd been involved in several business ventures, one being a pilot on a small boat on the Red and Mississippi Rivers. He had also run a store in Louisiana. Jackson had killed one man and wounded another in a fight and was proving hard to corral. He was finally captured for the handsome reward on his head, but the men who guarded him were not careful and he escaped. He fled to Shelby County, Texas, where there were no extradition laws, and then sent for his family.

This was a place for the Jackson family to grow. However, from the first, he was taken aback by the way the old guard rode herd like feudal lords over the valley. With the likes of men like Goodbread backed by other businessmen's interests, hired thugs, duplicitous land deals, and especially counterfeited headright certificates, it was difficult to settle. Besides intimidation, this old guard was engaged in a thriving rustling operation. The two factions were beginning to polarize, and outspoken Jackson became an important voice. He ran for the Texas Congress, hoping to settle the injustices legally, but he was checked by the local power brokers. He wrote and sent detailed letters to state officials and penned editorials to newspapers highlighting the problems in Sabine.

By April 1841, the land pirates had had enough of this troublesome gadfly and sent a man to shoot him. When Jackson returned to his house in the evening, a shot was fired from the woods. Luckily Jackson was only nicked on the hand, and he shrugged off the incident. Several days later, Jackson got a letter from Goodbread, telling him to stick to his own business or he'd kill him. The Jacksons showed the letter to a friend, as well as the scab where the bullet had grazed him. The friend had also mentioned that he'd recently had a falling-out with Goodbread. Jackson was never one to back down from a fight, and Goodbread's letter was the same as calling him out. Mrs. Jackson shared her husband's feelings, saying, "that he had had to kill rascals all his life and she expected he would have to kill a few more before they would let him alone."

Jackson is reportedly to have said, "He shan't live. He shan't." A friend of the Jackson's, the newly appointed Sheriff Alfred George, who was not Goodbread's friend, sent word to Jackson that Goodbread was unarmed at the corral. Riding his mare permitted Jackson to get the drop on Goodbread, who tried to talk his way out of the incident, explaining that he was unarmed. Jackson supposedly said, "So much the better." While his honor had been violated, Jackson wasn't about to dignify their differences with

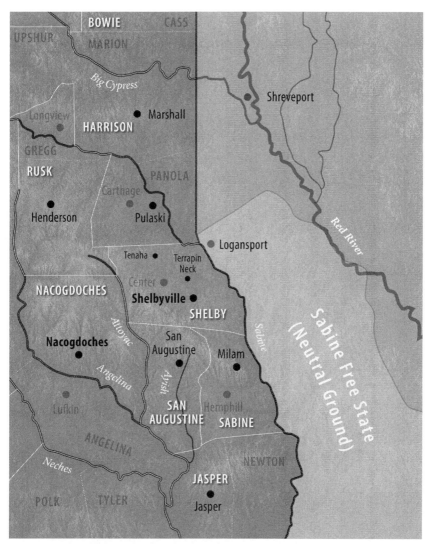

Area of the Regulator-Moderator War in East Texas, 1839–1844. At the center is Shelby County, where the conflict began. The surrounding counties were formed at the end of the war; white county names and borders represent the counties and county boundaries in 1846; gray place-names only appeared later. ZIETZ, CC BY-SA 4.0 <HTTPS://CREATIVECOMMONS.ORG/LICENSES/BY-SA/4.0>, VIA WIKIMEDIA COMMONS.

an honorable duel, a fight man to man; this was an execution. In Jackson's mind, Goodbread had been tried and convicted. Jackson felt like he was shooting a rattlesnake off his front porch—a snake that tried to strike several times. Jackson dodged the bites, picked up his rifle, and killed the threat.

Jackson turned himself in to his friend, Sheriff George, for murdering Goodbread. He was freed after his friends posted a $200 bond. Jackson had become a de facto leader. Fearing reprisals, his friends remained with him, and the Regulators were formed. But like so many vigilante movements, power can be intoxicating. In 1841 his case would be tried in Harrison County before Judge John Hansford. This was problematic, because neither Jackson nor the Regulators felt a fair trial was possible. Most knew the judge was a friend of the murdered Goodbread and, thus, sympathetic to the Moderator's cause. Intimidation was in order. On the day of Jackson's trial, pressing the issue, the armed Regulators showed up in force threatening to kill the judge if necessary. The Moderators, led by Ed Merchant, were caught off guard. The threat worked; Judge Hansford was no fool and fled. He left a note saying, "I'm not willing to risk my person in the courthouse." (Indeed, the threat was real; the judge would live a while longer before being shot by a Regulator mob.) In retaliation, the Moderators ambushed Jackson and a bystander. Charles Moorman became the commander and led raids on the Moderators, balancing the scale and reclaiming their sullied honor after Jackson was assassinated. And so began the bloodiest feud in Texas, a turf war that lasted nearly four years and choked several counties in East Texas. Each raid or murder necessitated a retaliatory hit. The year 1841 was a bloody beginning. Bill McFadden, John McFadden, and Squire Humphries were lynched by Regulators. Ambush and assassination were tools of terror; it's hard to overlook the deadly effect of a shotgun up close, but a rifle fired anonymously from cover is the safest bet. Adding to the 1841 death toll, Goodbread and Jackson, as well as Sheriff John Campbell, Daniel Minor, D. Morriss, and two men with the last names of Bledsoe and Lour need to be included. There were certainly others. This list does not account for men severely beaten by mobs; men who were shot and recovered; men shot whose limbs were amputated; destroyed property, burned homes and barns; stolen livestock; or lost business opportunities. We can't measure the pain and suffering of family members, grieving widows and children, or those who lost all their earthly possessions. This all occurred before the calendar turned to 1842, but there was more to come. During August 1844, several hundred Moderators and sixty Regulators met for a pitched battle. Fortunately, there were few fatalities. Governor Sam Houston sent the state militia to enforce peace. Also rumors about the delusional Regulator Commander, Charles Moorman, considering a coup d'état so he could be president of Texas were taken more seriously.

AFTERMATH

Hard feelings lingered for many years. The Mexican War became a larger threat, and many East Texans put differences aside for a time as they fought together, but old scars are not easily healed. At least thirty people were killed, but the number was surely higher. It would be good to report that the men and women of the Texas learned valuable lessons because of the Regulator-Moderator conflict, but they did not.

2

JOSEPH SMITH

AN AMERICAN PROPHET MURDERED BY AN AMERICAN MOB

I am like a huge, rough stone rolling down from a high mountain. The only polishing I get is when some corner gets rubbed off by . . . striking with accelerated force against religious bigotry.

—Joseph Smith

CARTHAGE, ILLINOIS AND NAUVOO, ILLINOIS, 1844

On June 27, 1844. Joseph Smith, the Mormon Prophet, was murdered on the second story of a stone jailhouse in Carthage, Illinois. It was a hot, humid day. The windows were open to catch a breeze. Smith, his brother, Hyrum Smith, and John Taylor had taken off their jackets and loosened their collars. Dr. Willard Richards still had his coat on. The jailer, worried about their safety, generously offered his comfortable bedroom upstairs instead of keeping the four men in the main cell on the first floor. There had been death threats against them, so it was appreciated. Earlier that day, a concerned Cyrus Wheelock slipped Joseph a pepperbox pistol, a percussion-cap revolver with six barrels. Another friend left a single-shot pistol for Hyrum.

Late in the afternoon, there was a commotion in the yard below. A concerned Dr. Richard looked out the window and saw "a hundred men storming the jail." Their faces were blackened by mud and wet gunpowder.

When the mob discovered Joseph and Hyrum were not in the cell on the main floor, there were vulgar, drunken shouts. These were followed by the chaos of fumbling footsteps and rifle barrels banging against the walls as all the vigilantes attempted to rush up the narrow staircase at once.

Joseph and the others barred the door with their bodies. When the mob at the top of the stairs couldn't shove the door open, someone anxiously fired a bullet through the keyhole, presumably to break the lock. It narrowly missed the men. Then, a second shot was fired through the panel of the door. The ball hit Hyrum squarely in the face. The ball entered below his left eye and exited on the right side under his chin. Presumably Hyrum had bent down to brace the door with his left shoulder, with his face understandably turned sideways. As Hyrum recoiled backward, another bullet entered his left side. As it exited, it flattened the watch in his right vest pocket. Hyrum fell to the floor saying, "I am a dead man."

Joseph cried out, "Oh, dear brother Hyrum!" Shielding his body, Joseph opened the door and fired the pepperbox randomly at the mob. He pulled the trigger six times—three of the six barrels discharged. Three men in the hall were wounded. Taylor reported, "The firing of Brother Joseph made our assailants pause for a moment; very soon after, however, they pushed the door some distance open, and protruded and discharged their guns into the room." Taylor and Dr. Richards "parried" the rifles with their walking sticks. Hoping he might escape, Taylor rushed for the window fifteen feet away, but a rifle ball hit him in the left thigh. He fell against the windowsill breaking the watch in his vest, which stopped at 5:16. Taylor cried, "I am shot!" Crumpling to the floor, he attempted to roll under the bed but not before he was shot three more times—in the knee, arm, and thigh. The round in the thigh ripped off a chunk of flesh the size of an orange. The mob poured into the room. For good measure, they shot the dead Hyrum, again.

Joseph, hoping to save his friend Dr. Richards, leapt to the window, drawing the mob's fire. He was the real target. Richard wrote, "Joseph was shot in the back two times. He also took bullets from the yard as he went out the window. Falling, he yelled, "Oh Lord, my God!" Richards felt Smith was dead when he hit the ground. An eyewitness, however, disagreed. William Daniels said Smith was still alive after he hit the yard below the window. In fact, Daniels claims Smith tried to lift himself up, but an impromptu firing squad propped him against a well and finished the job. After Dr. Richards tended to Taylor's wounds, he sent word to Nauvoo that Joseph and Hyrum were dead.

The next day, June 28, 1844, the corpses were placed in rough coffins and taken to Nauvoo. The wagon beds were covered with branches and straw to keep off the sun because the bodies were already starting to decompose. George Q. Cannon, a Nauvoo furniture maker who doubled as an undertaker, helped prepare and wash the bodies. The summer heat required that they move quickly. There was no way to mask the .54 caliber bullet hole on Hyrum's left cheek. Before the family viewing, Joseph and Hyrum were placed in a sitting position while wood frames were constructed around their faces to hold the molds for death masks. When Emma Smith saw his body, she's reported to have said, "Oh, Joseph, Joseph! My husband, my husband! Have they taken you from me at last!" The bodies laid in state at the Mansion House on June 29, 1844. More than ten thousand people paid their respects.

Newspaper reports were naturally polarized. The *New York Weekly Herald* reported, "Beyond the vineyards of Hancock County, beyond that beautiful bend in the Mississippi, he was a respected and an admired Prophet and statesman." The Reverend William G. Brownlow of the *Jonesborough Whig*, however, did not mince words. He said, "Smith was killed, as he should have been. THREE CHEERS to the brave company who shot him to pieces!" Alexander Campbell, a minister of the Campbellite movement, suggested the murder was the Lord's will. In his paper, the *Millennial Harbinger*, he wrote, "God cut him off by outlaws . . . the assassination of one whose career was in open rebellion against God and man."

Since 1830, The Church of Jesus Christ of Latter-day Saints— informally known as Mormons—had been driven from New York, Ohio, and Missouri. Now intolerance surged in Illinois. The plan was simple enough: Kill the leader or founder, so kill the movement. At times the struggle had been a turf war, but it had always been a battle for religious freedom guaranteed in the Bill of Rights. Although probably the most chronicled religious minority of the nineteenth century, the Church of Jesus Christ of Latter-day Saints was not alone. Other faiths also felt the oppression of religious intolerance as the nation struggled to build a more perfect union from less-than-perfect people. Catholics, Jews, American Indians, Africans, and Asians would be examples. Apparently, the devil was in the details. It seemed *tolerance* was a confusing issue when woven into a fabric of sectarianism, Manifest Destiny, and nationalism. When a belief system becomes politically predisposed to purging, vigilantism, inquisition, or debt slavery and enforces conversions, retaliations, and mob justice by physical or legal violence, say amen to civil rights. It's always been easier to dream about a promised land than to build one. The tenet about "loving your neighbor" appears to have categorical exclusions. Religious persecution is a special form of terror. In this chapter we'll examine Joseph Smith and explore why he was called the American Prophet. We'll also focus on how his teachings were revolutionary, why they threatened traditional religion, and why he ran for president of the United States.

KILLING THE LEADER

Live and let live is a difficult concept. The governor of Illinois, Thomas Ford, had offered his personal protection if Joseph Smith went to Carthage, the county seat, to face a charge of civil disobedience. The Prophet's experience with the machinations of "due process," as well as the promises from state and federal officials, had not been reassuring. He had good reason to fear for his life. Governor Ford formally mandated that Smith appear at Carthage or he would send a state militia to arrest him in Nauvoo. Governor Ford further stated he would not be responsible for the loss of life or collateral damage to the city, and he would repeal Nauvoo's City charter. Joseph and Hyrum felt the charges were unjust and politically motivated and that they could have been resolved in a more orderly, less dramatic fashion. This appeared to be a not-so-veiled attempt to remove the Prophet from his stronghold. Certainly, the Nauvoo Legion, the largest and best-trained militia in the state, could make mincemeat out of any state militia Governor Ford sent, but Joseph Smith knew he was in a precarious position. Yes, he was the mayor of Nauvoo, the largest city in Illinois, but he was also a General of the Nauvoo Legion. Governor Ford, therefore, was his immediate supervisor. No matter what legal saber-rattling existed between Mayor Smith and Governor Ford, the Nauvoo Legion had been chartered by the state. Thus, if Joseph Smith, as the general, called it up to defend either his person or the City of Nauvoo against a state militia sent by the governor—even if the charges against him were false—it would be an act of treason, a capital offense.

To keep the state militia out of Nauvoo, Joseph went to Carthage. He arrived around midnight and lodged at the Hamilton Hotel. The next morning, June 25, 1844, he met with Governor Ford. In the afternoon, Augustine Spencer and Henry Norton swore that Joseph Smith and his brother, Hyrum, were guilty of treason; the justice of the peace arrested them. Because there was no bail, the men were confined in the Carthage jail to await trial. Governor Ford left Carthage to go to Nauvoo. The Carthage Greys, instead of the more impartial state militia, had been assigned to guard the Mormon prisoners. As one Carthage Grey militiaman told several Latter-day Saints as they were leaving town, "We have had too much trouble to bring Old Joe here to let him ever escape alive, and unless you want to die with him you had better leave before sundown . . . and you'll see that I can prophesy better than Old Joe."

We don't know who shot Joseph Smith. Dr. Willard Richards and John Taylor made a list of people they recognized in the mob. In October 1844, nine men were indicted for the murders. In May 1845, five of those men were tried—Thomas C. Sharp, Levi Williams, Jacob C. Davis, Mark Aldrich, and William N. Grover—but all were acquitted. The Nauvoo Charter was revoked, and the Saints fled to the Rocky Mountains.

MARGINS OF RELIGIOUS TOLERANCE

The American colonies who established "plantations of religious freedom" often demonstrated an inconvenient truth: They had little patience with diverging theology. We often point to the Puritans, radical religious reformers who suffered great intolerance. Attempting to "purify" themselves in the New World, some were merciless about punishing sin and rooting out heretics. They targeted Quakers, Baptists, Anabaptists, and most of all, Catholics. Hanging four Quakers, including a woman, in less than ten years, served as an object lesson. Adultery, like apostasy, was a capital offense. Liberal thinking in early Massachusetts villages wasn't a healthy cultural fit. Thus, we see William Penn founding Pennsylvania as a haven for Quakers. Roger Williams's ideas about church and state were too liberal for Puritan tastes. He founded Rhode Island, as well as the Baptist Church. Lord Baltimore, with the help of his son, fostered a refuge for Catholics in Maryland. Each colony developed its own brand of Christianity, and some were more tolerant than others. Catholics were especially disliked. An illustration of the latter is this historical anecdote. Benedict Arnold's betrayal in the American Revolution, in part, was based on General George Washington's and the Continental Congress' negotiating with a Catholic France. In anger, Arnold claimed they had betrayed the "Reformation."

Although our nation's founders could not agree on slavery, they agreed with Roger Williams about separating church from state. Williams argued there needed to be a "hedge of separation" between the "wilderness of the world" and the "garden of the church." Thomas Jefferson agreed, writing "No man shall be compelled to frequent or support any religious worship, place, or ministry whatsoever, nor shall . . . suffer, on account of his religious opinions or belief." James Madison concurred, "The Religion then of every man must be left to the conviction and conscience." These opinions were reflected in the Bill of Rights, in theory, guaranteeing religious freedom.

THE SECOND GREAT AWAKENING

In the 1820s, the United States was transformed by what has been called the Second Great Awakening. This sweeping religious movement was more than a makeover for Protestant Christianity, however; it was a renewal that redefined spiritual worship, the nature of God, and the state of man. In many ways, it was also a romantic reaction against traditional Calvinism. This movement rejected the formal dogmas taught at the Harvard Divinity School, as well as other brands of institutional learning. Doctrines such as "predestined" salvation or the "natural depravity" of humankind didn't fit the new nation's model of an enlightened, secular self-government or a burgeoning rough frontier culture. Neither did the strict Calvinist tenet referred to as the "election of grace," meaning God would only save a few of his most select children. Strict Calvinism was "determinism," meaning all actions, events, and human behavior were determined by God.

The Second Great Awakening embraced a more inviting, more issue-driven concept called "free will." Men and women were free to make their own choices. Such thinking was influenced by the German philosopher Immanuel Kant, who argued that thinking can transcend "traditional constructs." In other words, humans don't need highly trained preachers, organized catechisms, stodgy dogmas, or rigid religious hierarchy to have religious experiences. Rather, a man, woman, or child can have a personal connection, even a personal relationship, with God. Why? Men and women are basically good.

A PROPHET OF THE GREAT AWAKENING

Joseph Smith was born on December 23, 1905, in Sharon, Vermont. His parents were hardworking, modest farmers, who often suffered from crop failures. When Joseph was ten, the Smith family moved to the Finger Lakes region of New York. By all accounts, they were a close, happy family, centered in their Christian faith. The children were schooled at home where Joseph learned how to read, write, and do basic math. His mother, Lucy Mack Smith, said Joseph was cheerful, intelligent, and contemplative. He would not be considered well-educated, but he had a basic literacy and could read the Bible.

When he was fourteen, in spring 1820, he wrote there "was an unusual excitement on the subject of religion." Starting with the Methodists, this religious fervor "became general among the various Christian sects." A young Joseph, concerned about his soul and salvation, wasn't sure which church he should join. He writes, "the whole district . . . seemed affected by it, and great multitudes united themselves to the different religious parties." He was confused because converting people to the different faiths seemed to be a contest that "created no small stir and division amongst the people." It bothered him that the good feelings that Christians should have for one another "were lost in a strife of words and a contest about opinions."

The local Baptists and Methodists were especially active. Northwest New York from Buffalo to Lake Erie was so heavily drenched with wandering itinerant preachers, circuit riders, revivals, and frontier-styled camp meetings that it was referred to as the "burned-over district." The "awakening" was hitting a fevered pitch, "flaming" with religious enthusiasm. The teenage Joseph, amid this theological milieu, was targeted for conversion by several preachers. He turned to his Bible where he found James 1:5, "if you lacked wisdom, ask God who gives to all men liberally." So, he slipped away into the forest, knelt, and prayed vocally, asking God which church to join. In the grove of trees, he records that he saw a pillar of light descending above the brightness of the Sun. God the Father and Jesus Christ appeared, telling him to join none of the churches because they were all wrong. As an excited young boy naturally would, he shared the experience with his supportive family. He was surprised and disappointed, however, when he shared what is called "the first vision" with local clergy. Instead of having his spiritual discovery celebrated, he was publicly castigated and personally attacked. He was told his vision was of the devil. Joseph recalls that his story "caused a great deal of prejudice against him." He said he found it strange that "an obscure boy" could be the lightning rod for "the most bitter persecution and reviling."

Again, Joseph was confused. He was told he could and should seek a religious experience, but a vision like he experienced was too much. Even for an awakened, transcendental Protestant, the heavens were closed to these kinds of visions and revelations—apparently, religious experiences had to be within accepted constructs. Stubbornly, Joseph said, "He knew he'd seen a vision and knew that God knew it." Dodging the verbal lashings from "those who ought to be my friends" in the religious community, he didn't join their churches. Rather, he waited for further direction from God. Religious freedom, he discovered, had limits.

THE BOOK OF MORMON

Three years later, on September 23, 1823, while Joseph was praying for a divine manifestation, his room filled with light. An angel who said his name was Moroni stood in the air near his bedside. Joseph said, "his countenance was like lightening." Moroni said he was from God and told Smith about a book written on thin, gold plates hidden on a mountain not far away. Moroni explained to Joseph that like the Bible, *The Book of Mormon* was another witness of Jesus Christ. It was a record of an ancient people who lived in the Americas, containing "the fulness of the gospel," and included Christ's visit after his crucifixion. Moroni told him when the time came, he would translate the plates by the gift of God. The next day, under the angel's direction, Joseph visited the location. Four years later, on September 22, 1827, Joseph was told to take the golden plates and translate them into English. The first edition of *The Book of Mormon* was published in March 1830. On April 6 of that year, Smith organized the Church of Jesus Christ of Latter-day Saints in Fayette, New York. However, the persecution only intensified.

AMERICAN PROPHET

For a better perspective on why Smith has been called an American Prophet, we will look at the observations of a contemporary of Smith's, the famous lawyer and future mayor of Boston, Josiah Quincy. Then we will look at what Harold Bloom, an influential critic of the twentieth century, proposed.

Quincy and his cousin, Charles Francis Adams, the son of John Quincy Adams, toured the American West in spring 1844. By chance, they made an unplanned stop at Nauvoo, Illinois, where Quincy spent the day with the Mormon Prophet. One of the great intellects of his day, Quincy was a Harvard-trained lawyer, a gifted speaker, and a writer. He was born to wealth and privilege. Before he met Joseph, he had been president of the Boston City Council and the president of the Massachusetts Senate. Later he would serve as mayor of Boston for three terms. Quincy wrote ten pages in his journal about his Nauvoo experience, as well as a detailed letter to his wife. Later, he would publish it as an article about Smith. In a rhetorical observation, Quincy posed a question and then answered it. He asked who had exerted the most powerful influence on the nineteenth century and the destiny of his country? His response was: It is by no means impossible that the answer to that interrogatory may be thus written: Joseph Smith, the Mormon Prophet. And the reply, absurd as it doubtless seems to most men now living, may be an obvious commonplace to their descendants.

Historically, Quincy's perspectives about Smith are unique for the modern reader because his observations are candid and sometimes sharp, but they are written by a disinterested party. Quincy had no political, religious, or economic agenda to promote. He was simply visiting an interesting man and writing about it.

Quincy was accustomed to civilization and its genteel refinements. He found the West dirty, muddy, and dusty. On one long stretch of the river trip, he saw only two houses he thought might be comfortable. He told his wife many of the men he saw looked like "miserable wood choppers." His first impression of Nauvoo wasn't positive. His first impression of Joseph Smith wasn't much better. When he was introduced, Smith was standing with a "crowd of loafers," and Quincy wasn't sure who was who. Finally, someone pointed out, "that's Joseph, the Mayor of Nauvoo, the General of the Legion, the Prophet of God." It was not a banner first impression! Quincy commented that Joseph was wearing dirty white pants and a tasteless checkered "speckled coat" and had a three-day growth of beard. After a while, however, his opinion started to change. Quincy commented that he soon realized that Smith was an "extraordinary" man of "rugged power."

He didn't believe that Smith had a divine calling, "The power he exercises both civilly & [sic] religiously is immense & is a living proof of the insceptibility [sic] of human nature to imposition." But he was impressed by Joseph's charisma and leadership. As a Whig, Quincy had serious reservations about the church's theocratic method of leadership; he preferred a healthy separation of powers. Quincy wanted his world organized and orderly—with God securely in his heaven where he belonged. "We passed the whole day," Quincy wrote, "in his society, & [sic] had one of the most extraordinary conversations I ever participated in, he preached for us, prophesied for us, interpreted hieroglyphics for us." For this Boston lawyer, here was a common uncommon man of the people, a man of the soil, a populist religious leader who could have been a romantic character in a novel, like Natty Bumppo from the *Leatherstocking Tales*. Quincy recognized that only in the American melting pot could a Boston Brahmin and a plowboy prophet meet on such equal terms.

Portrait of Joseph Smith Jr. PUBLIC DOMAIN.

They had much in common, yet they were separated by a world of differences. They shared a mutual respect. Quincy wrote to his wife, "I have neither time nor space to describe the faith or works of this most extraordinary man but reserve them for a future occasion." He called Smith in another reference, a backhanded compliment, a "Prophet, Priest, and King." Nothing, however, impressed Quincy more than a trip to the construction site of the Nauvoo Temple. He commented it was "a wonderous structure, altogether indescribable."

Harold Bloom was a Sterling Professor of Humanities at Yale University and certainly one of the most important literary critics in the last hundred years. In his book *The American Religion*, published in 1992, he makes several important observations about Smith. "I marvel at his intuitive understanding of the permanent religious dilemmas of our country." He continues by saying there is "no one like him in our national history." As a professed nonbeliever, Bloom makes the point that "Smith becomes almost a mythology in himself," arguing what "matters most . . . is how American both the man and his religion have proved to be."

He quotes R. Laurence Moore's observation in *Religious Outsiders and the Making of Americans*, suggesting that a traditional European Christian faith doesn't fit the American experience or the European culture because Americans prefer their own originals, such as Emily Dickinson, Walt Whitman, Herman Melville, Henry James, or Abraham Lincoln. "Mormons," Bloom continues, reflecting again on Moore, "taught American Religion, or at least a vital aspect of it . . . and provided a domestic alternative to faiths imported from Europe." This faith, he explained, followed a path that was uniquely American—which was reinventing themselves "out of a sense of opposition." Mainstream American theology, Bloom says is not "fixed." The Saints, by stepping out of mainstream American religion, "define themselves as being apart from the mainstream, Mormons were in fact laying their claim to it. By declaring themselves outsiders, they were moving to the center."

Harold Bloom argues that Smith's "King Follett Sermon," preached shortly before he was murdered, is "one of the truly remarkable sermons preached in America." Several concepts Smith preached in his three-hour sermon were considered so blasphemous that he should not be allowed to live. He taught that (1) God was once a man who has progressed to exaltation: "God himself was once as we are now, and is an exalted man, and sits enthroned in yonder heavens;" (2) matter and elements are eternal: "The pure principles of element are principles which can never be destroyed; they may be organized and re-organized, but not destroyed;" and (3) religious freedom should be available to all: "Meddle not with any man for his religion: all governments ought to permit every man to enjoy his religion unmolested."

OTHER PRINCIPLES JOSEPH SMITH TAUGHT

As both Quincy and Bloom noted, there were large differences between the teaching of the Mormon prophet and the traditional doctrines of Christianity. Such differences were not simply noticeable; they were uncomfortably noticeable, and incited persecution throughout his life. Smith preached a dynamic deity that was considered blasphemous to a traditional theist. God was not an amorphous mass of spiritual light and truth, and he was not incomprehensible three-in-one trinity. Rather, he preached that Heavenly Father had a literal son, Jesus Christ, and they were separate and distinct heavenly personages with a body of flesh and bones. This father-and-son relationship logically implied that there was a heavenly Mother, which was a difficult doctrine in his day. This Godly union "procreated" the spirit bodies of the human family who were born to Earth. As noted in the King Follett sermon, Joseph taught that God the Father and God the Mother were once a man and woman who at one time lived on an Earth like ours and who hand-in-hand progressed into Godhood. "As man is, God once was, as God now is, man may be."

The narrow definition of a "thumbs up" heaven or a "thumbs down" hell was also redefined. Although Joseph taught there was a literal heaven and a hell, it was unlike the traditional Christian beliefs that suggested some make it to heaven and that the rest will go to hell. Smith preached that most of the human family will qualify for "degrees of glory," the glory of the Sun, the Moon, or the stars. He emphasized that this church was not created from a few points of doctrine, for example, baptism by immersion. Rather, the church was restored by the authority of God through heavenly messengers, such as John the Baptist, Peter, James, and John, Elias, Elijah, and others.

MOVING TO THE FRONTIER

In the 1830s and 1840s, the Midwest was the frontier. Rather than fight the intolerance and persecution, it was easier to move the church to the frontier with the hope they could live in peace. From New York, the church moved to Kirtland, Ohio. While in Ohio, Smith felt God wanted him to build a "New Jerusalem," in Independence, Missouri, in Jackson County. Religious differences surfaced. There were issues about the nature of God, the large Mormon population that formed an economic and political voting bloc, and of course, slavery. Missouri was a slave state settled by Southerners, whereas most of the Mormon settlers were from the North. An editorial in the Mormon newspaper, *The Evening and*

Morning Star, written by W. W. Phelps in July 1833, further inflamed the non-Mormons in Jackson County. The article discussed alternatives to slavery. The Missouri residents felt the Latter-day Saints were no longer compatible neighbors. They wrote a public declaration that demanded the Mormon settlers remove themselves from Jackson County before spring 1834 or they would be removed by force. In Latter-day Saint history, this document is referred to as "The Missouri Mob Manifesto." The original petition has been lost, but it was printed in *The Evening and Morning Star* and referenced in regional newspapers during 1833:

> *We believe them [Mormons] to be deluded fanatics, or weak and designing knaves, and that they and their pretensions would soon pass away. . . . With very few exceptions they were of the very dregs of that society from which they came, lazy, idle, and vicious. . . . They openly blaspheme the Most High God, and cast Contempt on His holy religion. . . . we believe it a duty we owe to ourselves, our wives, and children to the case of public morals, to remove them from among us . . . [nor are we ready to have] the degraded and corrupted free negroes and mulattos that are now invited to settle among us. . . . They refuse to leave us in peace, as they found us, we agree to use such means as may be sufficient to remove them.*

The Latter-day Saints fled and moved to neighboring counties, and many lost their property. Several years later, in 1838, however, violence surged again. In Gallatin, Missouri, mobs of Missouri men barred the Latter-day Saints from voting. This was the beginning of what was called the Mormon War in Missouri. Farms and properties were burned, people murdered, and women raped. One example was Amanda Barns, who watched as a Missouri ruffian put a gun in her son's mouth and pulled the trigger. Another man said something about it being a damn shame to kill the boy. The man who pulled the trigger said, something like nits make lice.

The Latter-day Saints were forced to flee in the winter, with many leaving with what they could carry in their arms. The Missouri Governor Lilburn Boggs's signed Executive Order 44, often called "The Mormon

TARRING AND FEATHERING OF JOSEPH SMITH.

A mob tarring and feathering Joseph Smith. PUBLIC DOMAIN/WIKIMEDIA COMMONS.

Extermination Order." Governor Boggs directed Missouri Militia General John B. Clark to action. "The Mormons," Boggs ordered, "must be treated as enemies, and must be exterminated or driven from the state. . . . you are authorized to do so to any extent you may consider necessary." The church was forced from the state of Missouri, in the middle of winter, at gunpoint.

THE LIBERTY JAIL
Smith and his associates were arrested on November 1, 1838. General Joseph Doniphan was ordered to take the men to the square and shoot

them the next morning. Doniphan, however, refused the direct order, stating such an act would be murder. He turned the men over to a civil court. On December 1, 1838, awaiting trial, Joseph Smith, Hyrum Smith, Sidney Rigdon, Lyman Wight, Caleb Baldwin, and Alexander McRae were incarcerated in the Liberty Jail to await trial for high treason. The conditions in the Liberty Jail were akin to a cell in a concentration camp. The jail cell was 14 by 14½ feet and was entered through a trapdoor from the main level. There were two narrow, barred windows near the ceiling that provided the only light. Little wonder that Joseph would cite prison reform in his presidential platform. Smith recorded, "We are kept under a strong guard, night and day . . . we have been compelled to sleep on the floor with straw, and not blankets sufficient to keep us warm."

For four months during a bitterly cold winter, the men were kept in intolerable conditions. Under the pretext of going to Boone County for trial, the guards allowed the Mormon leaders to escape. In fact, while several of the guards drank whiskey, one man helped the emaciated men saddle the horses. Because the charges would not hold up in court, political leaders saved face by allowing them to escape.

JOSEPH VISITS WASHINGTON, DC

Smith went to Washington, DC, seeking redress for the Latter-day Saints' losses in Missouri. He visited Congress and President Martin Van Buren. His efforts proved fruitless. Although it was impossible to put a price tag on human suffering, the pecuniary value, on the petition Smith presented to the United States was $2 million. President Van Buren told Smith his "cause was just but there was nothing he could do." Van Buren had championed personal liberties in the past, but he also understood the political tightrope on which he was balanced. His political agenda was "preserving the Union." Slavery being "the" explosive issue of his day, he argued that the federal government must not interfere with states. Smith felt the president treated him with disrespect. Congress was a little more circumspect, saying it was "a state, not a federal issue." Henry Clay said, "You better go to Oregon." John Calhoun said, "It's a nice question—a critical question, but it will not do to agitate it."

There is a humorous anecdote about the Smith-Van Buren meeting. I hope it is true. On April 17, 1840, *The Peoria Resister*, reported that Smith "told the president he was getting fat. The president replied that he was aware of the fact; that he had to go every few days to the tailors to get his clothes let out or to purchase a new coat. The "prophet" here added, at the top of his voice, 'he hoped he would continue to grow fat, and swell, and, before the next election burst!'"

THE LATTER-DAY SAINTS IN ILLINOIS

Joseph and the Latter-day Saints hoped Nauvoo would be different, and for a time, it was; but the tide of public opinion was turning, and religious persecution began to intensify. The rapid growth of Nauvoo apparently posed not only an economic but a political threat to the other towns in the county. For example, as early as 1841, John Sharp, the editor and owner of the *Warsaw Signal* (formerly known as *Western World*), took aim and fired editorial salvos at the Mormons. He felt that Warsaw, twenty miles to the south, would be impacted. According to the 1840 county census, there were 2,450 in the Nauvoo precinct. The number would double in a year. Early in 1841, Sharp wrote, "Mormon ascendancy in this county . . . the church can exercise such an all-powerful influence over his [Joseph Smith] deluded followers . . . what may . . . become of your dearest rights and most valued privileges, when that ascendancy is made."

On May 6, 1842, the ex-governor of Missouri, Lilburn Boggs, the man responsible for the Extermination Order, was shot at his home in Independence, Missouri. He was reading the paper after dinner when a would-be assassin fired a large pistol loaded with buckshot. Several balls hit Boggs in the head, and another hit his throat. Doctors thought the shots would be fatal, but Boggs recovered. Investigators found a stolen pistol near the window. Boggs wanted Smith extradited to Missouri. He put pressure on Illinois governor Thomas Carlin to issue warrants. Carlin issued them, and they were served by a Missouri undersheriff who left the men in the custody of the Nauvoo Marshal. However, Smith and Porter Rockwell were freed by Nauvoo Municipal Court, which had the power to grant writs of habeas corpus. The officers with the warrants didn't recognize the court's authority, so Smith and Rockwell went into hiding.

In January 1843, Smith was defended by the famous Whig trial lawyer Justin Butterfield, a champion of personal liberty and constitutional law. As an historical aside, Butterfield's associate, Stephen Douglas, would run against Abraham Lincoln. Previously Stephen Douglas had ruled favorably for the Latter-day Saints in an 1840 court case. Afterwards, he invited Joseph Smith to dinner. On the day of the trial, the infamous fugitive, Smith, defended by the famous Butterfield, walked into a packed courthouse. Butterfield, always a clever-witted showman, played to the ladies in the balcony and to the respected Judge Pope. He started by saying, "May it please your honor, I appear before the Pope, in the presence of angels, to defend the Prophet of the Lord."

He showed that Smith had not been in Missouri on the day that Boggs was shot and that hearsay was not evidence. Boggs needed proof for extradition. More importantly, this was a constitutional issue about whether a federal court had jurisdiction over a state court; specifically, could an Illinois resident, Joseph Smith, be extradited to Missouri if he had not fled his home state or because an ex-executive, Lilburn Boggs, with political pull, requested it? The outcome was the efficacy of the federal court, granted by Congress, over the state court. We must remember at this time, the states' rights were hotly contested, and at the heart of this debate was slavery and preserving the union.

JOSEPH SMITH'S PRESIDENTIAL PLATFORM

Somewhat jaded by the political process, and to protect the rights of the church, Smith decided to run for president of the United States. He said, "I feel it's my right and privilege to obtain what influence I can lawfully in the United States for the protection of injured innocence." It was a good way to get his message to many people. The Latter-day Saints were a large voting block and certainly the largest block of voters in Illinois. It's also interesting that by this time, he had become an outspoken abolitionist. He felt that any Black owned by a member of the church should be set free. "Come Texas; come Mexico; come Canada and come all the world—let us be brethren: let us be one great family; let there be world peace." His platform was simple:

1. Antislavery, end by 1850, compensated emancipation for slave owners, sales of public lands.

2. Establish a national bank, full reserve spending, capital stock owned by the federal government.

3. Tariff to protect agriculture, manufacture, and commerce

4. Reduce size of Congress, two members per million, would be more efficient.

5. Annex Texas, California, and Oregon

6. Reform prisons, abolish prisons and debtors' prisons. Rather make the penalty applicable to work on roads, public works, or any place where the culprit can be taught more wisdom and more virtue.

7. Have federal government protect minority rights like those of the Latter-day Saints and to seek protection from mob violence.

8. "The neighbor from any State or from any country, of whatever color, clime, or tongue, could rejoice when he put his foot on the sacred soil of freedom, and exclaim, the very name of 'America' is fraught with *friendship!*"

His campaign was cut short by his murder. He was the only presidential candidate to be assassinated while running for office.

THE LAST DAYS

Certain his days were numbered, Smith would fight for his beloved city. He wanted to live long enough to see the temple completed. In winter 1844, he met with the Twelve Apostles and made the following statement:

> *Send out a delegation & investigate the locations of [sic] California & oregon & find a good location where we can remove after the Temple is completed. & build a city in a day—and have a government of our own.*

3

JOHN GLANTON, SCALP HUNTER

THE GLANTON GANG TERRORIZES NORTHERN MEXICO

It was a cold, frosty morning. The scalped heads presented a very revolting spectacle. A peculiar vapor or steam ascended from them all. Many of these poor creatures were still alive, and groans were heard on all sides.

Ohio History, Volume 23

ARIZONA TERRITORY, 1850

It was a dangerous, bloody business venture, but a scalp was worth cash money. A handful could net a man more than he'd normally make in a year. Traditionally, a scalp was a warrior's battle trophy, a way of keeping score. To a bounty hunter, however, it was a receipt redeemable for services rendered. You couldn't say you killed an Indian until you proved it. John Glanton carefully instructed his men to include the ears with the crown before the scalp was salted and hung on a pole to dry. This proved that the scalp was not cut in half when Mexican officials examined it before authorizing payment.

The northern Mexican states had been plagued by Apache and Comanche raiders. As early as 1835, the controversial solution had been bounty hunters; the Mexican Army was too small to protect such a large frontier. One year, in a northern Mexican valley, a party of Comanche

Indians killed several hundred Mexicans and drove off hundreds of cattle. In other locations, the Apache Indians had become so bold that they were said to plunder larger towns during daylight hours. The state of Chihuahua paid $17,756 for scalps in 1849. For John Glanton, a former Texas Ranger, the money was too good to pass up; besides, he hated Indians and said he liked killing them. Hunting American Indians was more lucrative than working in the California goldfields—or his other job, which was robbing travelers. He held a commission by the state of Sonora and was paid 100 pesos for a brave, 50 pesos for a woman, and 25 pesos for a child, the standard rate. When the "hostile" Apache Indians were hard to find, neither Glanton nor his men were particular. A noncombative Indian's scalp looked like an Apache Indian's scalp—Yuma, Pima, Navajo—any scalp would do. For that matter, a dark-haired Mexican peasant worked, too. Glanton noted that killing Indians used to be easier. Back in the 1830s, the glory days of this profession, a man named Johnson had been able to make a small fortune rather quickly. He would entice the "savages" with trade items. When they bunched together to look at the trade items, he fired his cannon filled with shot, so there were plenty of bodies ready for scalping.

John Glanton was a historical character, but there is much we don't know. We are morbidly curious about his story—curious in the same way we're curious about venereal diseases, bubonic plague, or Jack the Ripper. We wonder about his psychological profile. It's safe to assume he had some sort of antisocial personality disorder, but what else drove him? How do people like Glanton, Nero, or Adolf Hitler evolve? Fear and violence are borderless; they move in and out of all cultures and dispensations. No society, ethnic group, or race is immune. Often violence and fear can be overlooked—sanitized by historians, a social system, or hidden in language constructions we don't stop to think about. For example, we're disgusted by Glanton the scalper, and rightly so. But we may not think twice about the Western bounty hunter or lawman who brings in a wanted man, draped over a saddle, who was "wanted dead or alive." Or we don't stop to consider the words of the famous gunfighter, Wild Bill Hickock. He was asked how many men he had killed in stand-up gunfights. In his

Thomas Millman, physician to the North American Boundary Commission, kept a diary of his experiences while in the West. On July 31, 1874, he wrote "we met with Boswell & Dawson & the photographers. They were getting the photo of some dead Indians. They appear to be Crow Indians killed last winter by the Pegans. About 20 altogether were riddled with bullet holes & every one scalped. Most of them had their shirts & every one had a gash in their side. Bodies were shrivelled up but skin pretty sound." PUBLIC DOMAIN/WIKIMEDIA COMMONS.

day, Wild Bill's reply would not have raised an eyebrow. "Well," he said with effect, "not counting Indians and Mexicans, I have killed [*x* number] of men." This meant real men, of course—that is, two white guys justifying their honor with Colts, shooting it out face-to-face on the street of a town. It was the only proper way for men of European decent to count coup. Apparently, too, the only good Indian was a dead Indian, and the Mexican population was a damned nuisance. When it came to notches on the barrel of your gun, dead was not dead.

We know some things about Glanton, but it is based on few historical facts. What we have are few subjective firsthand stories, mythology, and legend. We get blurry pieces of an image, but the mosaic is not complete. An example might be his death; several firsthand reports follow. In one thread, he was killed by the Yuma Indians by bashing his head with clubs; slitting his throat with trade knives; chopping him with hatchets; shooting him; or tying him to a pole with a dog and burning him on the banks of a river. The other threads suggest he was shot by white men he tried to rob or was killed by one of his own men. We know he worked for the Mexican state of Chihuahua, but Chihuahua officials got fed up with him and put a bounty on his head. Nevertheless, he was quickly hired by the state of Sonora, the officials of which felt they needed his services. He and his scalpers are supposed to have collected 250 scalps on one killing spree in the Big Bend Region. His body count was horrific, but like notches on a gunfighter's six-gun, the number of Galton's dead was, we hope, exaggerated. In this chapter, we'll look at the practice of scalping and then shift into several legendary and historical sketches—a quasi-biography from a man who said he rode the "scalp trail" with John Glanton.

THE SCALP HUNTING TRADE

To lift a scalp—usually the victim is dead—the scalper grabs a fistful of hair on the front of the victim's forehead, makes a circular cut around the clenched fist, and then pulls. It would be wrong to assume that scalping was a uniquely American practice. Indeed, a quick review shows it has a long history dating back at least five or six thousand years. There are ancient Scandinavian sites, for example, that show evidence of this practice. Historically there are records of the ancient Greeks taking scalps, and the practice also shows up in pre-Columbian cultures in the New World. There is evidence that the Chinese practiced scalping. It was also done in medieval England and, of course, by American Indians. In the early days of the Connecticut and Massachusetts colonies, bounties were paid for American Indian scalps. The practice continued but was far more common among American Indians. Scalp bounties were paid during the French and Indian and Revolutionary wars. Another example, much later, would occur at Sand Creek on November 29, 1864. Colonel John Milton Chivington, a Methodist pastor preached, "Damn anyone who sympathizes with Indians . . . I have killed Indians and believe it's right and tolerable." He led his soldiers at the infamous Sand Creek Massacre. Mostly old men, women, and children were killed. In fact, the old Cheyenne chief

Robert McGee, scalped by Sioux Indian Chief Little Turtle in 1864.
COURTESY OF LIBRARY OF CONGRESS.

even waved a flag of truce, but the soldiers were determined to have a victory. They collected many scalps, but they also collected other trophies, including human fetuses, as well as male and female genitalia for curios or coin purses. Some of the men cut the uteruses out of the women they'd kill; such trophies were slung over their saddle horns and paraded on the streets of Denver when they returned.

Because Mexican scalp bounties were paid as early as 1835 (the practice ended in the 1880s), a wide assortment of bounty hunters were employed, including runaway slaves, Seminole and Delaware Indians, and an assortment of Yankees. Perhaps the most famous was James Kirker (1795–1852). Kirker was born in Ireland but came to the United States sometime later. He was a mountain man and a trapper with William Henry Ashley in 1822. He became a Mexican citizen and began his long career hunting and killing Apache Indians for bounty money. During the Civil War, it was reported that Bloody Bill Anderson had a wall of "Northerner" scalps he liked to show off. As the western migration continued, a few communities harried by raids by American Indians raised funds in their "community chest" to hire bounty hunters to kill and scalp the offenders. Perhaps one of the most famous scalps was taken by Buffalo Bill Cody. He proudly lifted the "first scalp for Custer." It was taken from a Cheyenne Indian named Yellow Hair. Cody was always a promoter, and this action brought him fame in the national press and helped launch his wild west shows.

HOW DO WE KNOW JOHN GLANTON?

The core of John Glanton's story and the exploits of his gang have come in large part from a piece called *My Confession: The Recollection of a Rogue* by Samuel Chamberlain. Chamberlain was a Boston man who went West to find adventure. He fought in the Mexican War, likely deserted, and then rode with the Glanton Gang. He tells a bloody story in his sketch. It is a firsthand account in which the gang hunts down Apache Indians—and any other American Indian who got in their way. Chamberlain's account is interesting, and we get a picture of Glanton but one that isn't necessarily accurate. He's inconsistent and careless with names and dates, although some of his narrative is true. It's enough to make a person reach for a nausea bag. Chamberlain, however, finally left the gang and went on to have a normal life. He married well and during the Civil War, rose to the rank of brevet brigadier general. Chamberlain lived in Massachusetts until he died in either 1906 or 1908. Among other references, Glanton shows up in Jeremiah Clemens's *Bernard Life*, a novel about the Texas Revolution, published in 1856. Glanton also turns up in George MacDonald's *Flashman and the Redskins* in 1982. Without a doubt, however, Cormac McCarthy's novel *Blood Meridian*, published in 1985, makes Glanton more famous than the scalp hunter Kirker. McCarthy's book is fictional, but McCarthy is not only a brilliant writer but also a meticulous student of history. *Blood Meridian* is loosely based on Chamberlain's *My Confession: The Recollection of a Rogue*, but McCarthy's book takes on a life of its own. It's psychologically and physically violent—perhaps repulsively violent at times—but the book is about a psychopathic killer, a Western horror novel.

THE SHORT VIOLENT LIFE OF JOHN GLANTON

John Glanton was born in 1819 in Edgefield County, South Carolina. His family lived in several southern states before moving to Texas and putting down roots in Gonzalez. As a teen, he supposedly served in the Texas Revolution, but accounts vary. Reports suggest he was nearly killed in a battle and, at some point, fell in love. The girl of his dreams was captured during an Apache Indian raid. He and some of the men followed the Apache Indians but were too late to save his fiancé. She was raped, brutalized, and scalped. The heartbroken, traumatized young man vowed vengeance. Although this kind of tragedy surely occurred on the frontier, it feels like it might have been manufactured to explain Glanton's future brutality and hatred of Indians.

Later descriptions suggest Glanton had a violent temper. It's said he did something to Sam Houston but no details exist. But supposedly because Houston was livid, Glanton fled to Louisiana. At some point, he returned to San Antonio and possibly became a Texas Ranger. He fell in love again, but this time to a young lady named Joaquina, a "Texas beauty." They got married and started a family. He joined the volunteers during the Mexican War as a Texas Ranger. He is supposed to have fought bravely; he was one of the guerilla fighters in Mexico and participated in the slaughter of both Mexican soldiers and civilians alike. He was said to have killed a Mexican for his horse. In the Battle of Monterrey, he helped kill Mexican peasants. According to General Zachary Taylor, "There was not a crime the rangers did not commit."

GLANTON KILLED

After the war, Glanton left his wife and children for good and headed West. At first, he thought he might like to try his luck in the California goldfields but discovered there was more money in robbing and killing those en route to California. Chamberlain recalled the first day he joined the gang. Glanton was on his way to cash in some of the scalps when he came across a group from Sonora. Disguising themselves as Apache Indians, they raided the camp, killing and scalping three Mexicans and taking five women. Because three of the women were old and ugly, they killed them. The other women were raped and abused. During this "orgy," according to Chamberlain, the group was attacked by the Sonorans. The women they raped were killed; the five dead women were then scalped.

After other killing sprees, the gang traveled to the Colorado, where ferry services carrying travelers to California were making a lot of money. Glanton and his crew decided to cash in on the profits. One ferry service was operated by a man named Lincoln and the other by the Yuma Indians. The gang frightened Lincoln, so he left. Glanton took over the Yuma ferry, killing some of the Indian men and taking and raping nine of the Indian women. The Yuma Indians arrived in a huff. Glanton told them they needed to provide more women and food or he'd kill them. At this point, Samuel Chamberlain said he'd had enough. On April 23, 1850, before Chamberlain and others deserted, the Yuma Indians attacked and killed Glanton.

4

SAN FRANCISCO SEX TRAFFICKING IS ANOTHER GOLD RUSH

Allow me to express to your respected body our high appreciation of your valuable services. . . . But, gentlemen, one thing more must be done . . . for the good of those who remain, and as an example to others.
—From a letter to the San Francisco's Vigilance Committee about prostitution, 1856

SAN FRANCISCO, CALIFORNIA, 1850–1860

It was understood that a prostitute in Chinatown would have a professional life for four or five years before she was "worn out." Then she had options; specifically, she could choose how she would like to commit suicide, or she could be murdered. Her script had been written in advance and the final scene was never a surprise. However, because of disease, opium addiction, or a powerful will to live, a prostitute might delay the inevitable. She knew a proper Chinese woman should swallow her "existential angst" without complaint. Her world was a world of obedience and duty. As a woman who had little or no value in her culture, she could not bring honor to her family as a son might, but by doing her filial duty as a daughter, she would not bring dishonor. It's speculation, but maybe she had been taught there was some comfort in exiting into a kinder oblivion or perhaps she hoped she would cross that mystical silver bridge into a better world.

The most common method of suicide was eating raw opium, but there were other choices. It's likely that because her enslavement in the brothel, she had not stepped out of doors for years. At best she might have glimpsed a street or alley through barred windows. When her time came, she would be taken to a Chinese doctor who would determine her sentence. If she had no professional value, she could expect to be locked in a room about the size of a closet. She'd be given a cup of tea, a scoop of rice, and a small lamp. When the oil burned out, there would be darkness until she starved to death or committed suicide. She might improperly scream or pound on the door, but the walls were thick, and the apathy thicker. Her duty was to die properly and as expeditiously as she could. After several days had passed, her managers would return, expecting to find her corpse. If she wasn't dead, they could facilitate her passing, or if they were feeling charitable, they dropped her at a nearby street corner to die.

There are important stories that should be told about the Chinese migration to America. The first wave of immigrants were Chinese men who came to San Francisco; Chinese workers later spread throughout the West. A sometimes-overlooked part of this narrative deals with the immigration of women, women who for several decades were targeted for prostitution. This is not a comfortable story. These women, a good number of whom were teenagers, had been enslaved in China and shipped to service Chinese men in the United States. In the early boomtown days, most of these women worked in San Francisco in overcrowded Chinatown brothels; some were sold to white brothel keepers. A Chinese woman cost less than $50 in China; in California, however, she might be worth twenty times that amount. To flesh traffickers women were treated as cargo. Most were petrified, and many were young girls away from home for the first time. Like ships carrying enslaved African people, a predictable number would not survive the sea voyage—overcrowding, poor sanitation, and disease took their toll. It was "stack 'em deep and feed 'em cheap." Generally, this live cargo was kept in steel cages or wood boxes. Crew members raped the women because "humbling" or "breaking" them in during the sea voyage was a common practice.

THE CALIFORNIA GOLD RUSH

The discovery of gold can't be kept quiet. It was gold fever! Newspaper accounts suggested all a person needed to do was kick the dirt and look for nuggets. Gold fever not only fueled a migration across the United

Belle and Charles Cora House in San Francisco, 1853.
PUBLIC DOMAIN/WIKIMEDIA COMMONS.

States, it was world news, triggering an international migration—in addition to the hordes of Yankees rushing to California via overland routes or by sea. A sleepy bay village on the California coast suddenly became a major hub for the goldfields; overnight, San Francisco became a boomtown, hosting ten thousand men who planned on becoming millionaires within the month. Hammers and saws could be heard day and night as buildings were constructed. Growth was so rapid it took years for civil and legal infrastructure to catch up. It also took time to establish law and order. The early days were tooth and claw; fortunes were made and lost overnight. When there was an issue, it was handled by fist, axe handle, bowie knife, or pistol. As the saying goes, if in doubt, shoot first.

The dream, of course, was becoming rich, and we naturally think of a miner hitting the mother lode, but there were other corollary fortunes to be made—mostly by separating the miner or would-be miner from his gold or investment money. These paths included supplying prospectors with the equipment, supplies, investment capital, or other sundry items needed to prospect; providing diversions, specifically the three Ws, whiskey, women, and wagering; or taking what was desired by force or deceit.

For protection, many honest men often banded together as collectives, in associations, or along ethnic lines. Less ethical men formed criminal gangs. Some San Francisco districts like the Barbary Coast neighborhood were especially lawless. A group of Australian convicts invested in brothels, bars, and gambling joints. They called themselves the Sydney Ducks. The Ducks were not above beating up a lovesick man at a brothel for his gold dust or rolling a man for his pocket watch if he drank liberally. Another group formed, and many of the constituents were former military men from the Mexican War. This group called themselves the Hounds (later calling themselves Regulators); they ran brothels and vice joints. They, too, were not above beating up or murdering a man for his money. When a gang's business interests conflicted with another gang, there were wars. At times the Barbary Coast resembled a war zone. Adding to this the mix of rogues were the Chinese tongs, criminal gangs based in Chinatown.

THE GUM SAN HOPE: CHINESE MIGRATION TO CALIFORNIA

By the 1840s, China was facing severe economic depression, and people were starving. China had lost the Opium War to Great Britain and was forced to open its markets. This, coupled with years of poor crops and the Taiping Rebellion in the southeast, made domestic prospects grim. News about the gold rush in California had reached China. Young Chinese men looked to Gum San, the golden mountains of California, as an answer to their poverty. Gold fever called like a siren, singing a promise of economic salvation. Young men could go to the United States, find work, maybe find gold, and send money to their families. If fortune smiled, they might come home rich. An ocean voyage was expensive and frightening, but those who could scraped together the necessary funds by mortgaging family land or borrowing money from family. Others committed to years of servitude with brokers who specialized in bringing Chinese men to California. A worker's wages would be garnished until he'd served the years he committed to and his debt, with interest, was paid in full. Unscrupulous labor bosses who needed workmen sometimes kidnapped or "shanghaied" them.

Chinese, gold mining in California. THE BANCROFT LIBRARY, UNIVERSITY OF
CALIFORNIA, BERKELEY.

Like many Americans who came to California, Chinese men didn't
plan to stay; this was solely an economic venture. They would exploit the
resource and return home wealthier. But as so often happened, the land
itself, and the new possibilities it offered, were the real treasures. In 1850,
four thousand Chinese men were seeking their fortunes in the United
States, along with a handful of Chinese women. There was a need for
cheap labor in the California goldfields and later, as railroad workers. By
1853, there were nearly twelve thousand Chinese men in California. That
number would soon become sixty-five thousand men and five thousand
women. By the 1870s, arguably 25 percent of the California population
was Chinese. These Chinese were not enthusiastically welcomed by the
white population. They were paid 50 percent less than whites for identical
work, and often, they were assigned the most dangerous tasks. Many felt
that darker-skinned workers were expendable.

TARGETING SOJOURNERS IN A NEW LAND

Chinese immigrants considered themselves sojourners, temporary pilgrims in a strange land. They were an ethnocentric people with binding ties to Mother China. Indeed, if death overtook them on their pilgrimage, it was important that their bones be taken home for proper burial. The immigrants during the first few decades weren't interested in blending with Caucasian culture or society; the feeling was mutual. The Chinese, like Mexicans or American Indians, were not even second-class citizens. If the Celestials or Orientals, as Chinese were often called, knew their place in the social order, they were tolerated. They could do the menial jobs they were "destined" to do: laundry, cooking, or hard labor. A malignant racism became pronounced when the white population felt the Chinese were competing for jobs that should belong only to whites—especially jobs in the goldfields. It became an explosive subject. Racial slurs flew, but one railroad manager made a surprising comment, "they proved nearly equal to white men in the amount of labor they perform."

Reclaiming a Wild West San Francisco from criminal gangs and the lawless did not happen overnight. As concerned citizens and business interests established a working legal system, the city became partially domesticated. Sadly, however, law and order mingled with vigilante justice that targeted ethnic groups—Chinese, Mexicans, American Indians, and Irish. Orientals were proposed to be so immoral they would corrupt wholesome American values. M. B. Starr wrote *The Coming Struggle, or What the People on the Pacific Coast Think of the Coolie Invasion*. Starr's thesis is that Orientals are "heathen Sodomites and San Francisco is a large bordello." He added that "imported prostitution is endorsed by the Chinese government" and that Chinese women were a "moral threat" to decent people. Laws to limit foreigners and foreign competition were passed. The Miner's License Tax, for example, required non-natives (specifically targeted at Chinese, Mexicans, and American Indians) to pay $20 a month to work. This was onerous when a man's wages were only $7 a month. Still another law was enacted stating that no person of Chinese heritage could testify against a white man in court. To enforce these mandates, the state legislature passed a $50 tax on Asian immigrants. Editorials in the *Daily Alta California*, as early as 1853 debated "how white" could an Oriental be? One conclusion was the Chinese were "worse than negroes" because they were "deceitful," and there should be no association between the two races.

THE PROBLEM OF CHINESE PROSTITUTION

Increasing tension was building as more Chinese workers came to the United States. One of the issues was prostitution. Chinese men wanted Chinese women. But for the Northerners in the Bay Area, there was little difference separating the importation of Chinese women and importing Black slaves. Citizens complained about Chinese women who were illegally brought to San Francisco, and in 1860, police were pressured to act. They raided a ship and found mostly teenagers aboard who were promised to several local brothels; they were eight to eighteen years old. An observer commented that a Chinese prostitute in her twenties looked like she was an old woman, and a medical doctor observed that 88 percent of the women he examined had a venereal disease before they were twenty. An article in the *San Francisco Chronicle* suggested, "the importation of females [is] in bulk . . . each China steamer now brings consignments of women, destined to [be] placed on the market." By the 1870s, it was estimated that 85 percent of Chinese women in California were prostitutes. To traffickers, brothel owners, or men who paid for services rendered, such women were an expendable commodity, and if this kept the Chinese workforce happy, so be it.

Chinese women were not truly culturally valued, and in a time of famine they were a definite liability. Some families were willing to sell their daughters to sex brokers. Other families were willing to sell because the traffickers told them they were collecting women for Chinese husbands. Arranged marriages were common, and parents felt marriage was a better situation for their daughter. Occasionally, the time-proven method of kidnapping was employed. A young woman or girl could be procured for a few dollars and shipped to the United States.

CHINESE WOMEN SOLD ON THE BLOCK

The prettiest, most desirable women were sold privately to wealthy men as concubines or to high-end brothels. In 1869, the *San Francisco Chronicle* reported: "The particularly fine portions of the cargo, the fresh and pretty females who came from the interior, are used to fill special orders from wealthy merchants and prosperous tradesmen. A very considerable portion are sent . . . in answer to demands from well-to-do miners and successful vegetable producers."

The other women were placed in "barracoons" or holding cells comparable to those in the Antebellum South. They were cleaned up and placed on the auction block where they might be stripped and suffered physical examinations. If a prospective woman seemed willful, worried, or anxious, she would be drugged. In the first decade, most of the women would be sold to Chinese brothels as crib girls, although this kind of slavery was no respecter of persons or ethnicity because anyone with cash was welcome to make a bid.

THE TONGS WERE GANGSTER POLICE

Tongs are Chinese criminal gangs. They have a dark history and play a strong role in this story. They preyed on and exploited the vulnerable while making handsome profits. Sometimes they got along, and other times they did not. Their calling cards were intimidation, terror, and violence. Along with Chinese businessmen, local police, and corrupt officials, they made fortunes off prostitution, gambling, opium, and protection. For the most part, they were active inside the Chinese community—staying to themselves as much as possible—but where business interests were concerned, the streets could get bloody. As in any honor culture, intimidation, retaliation, and keeping face were pivotal. Tong enforcers were called *boo how doy*, and their job was to do the bloody, dirty work.

The *boo how doy* were practiced at backing up threats and terrorizing the Chinese community. They had a knack for head banging and brutality. Besides knives, a favorite weapon was a common hatchet with a short handle. It was a good weapon for close quarters—and, yes, the enforcers were referred to as "hatchet men." Essentially, the tongs made certain prostitution, among other crimes, ran smoothly. They were criminal police enforcing their own laws. With prostitution they were involved in every level of the business, from shipping, payoffs, and auctioning, to bill collection. If a woman escaped, which happened rarely, the tong would "recover" her. In this culture, it was not acceptable to go to the police; the tong were the police.

GETTING AROUND THE LAW

To get around California's antislavery laws and cloak the transaction with a semblance of legality, a Chinese woman would sign an "indenture" document that stated she knew what she was signing and was doing this of her own free will. Not knowing the language, we will assume her *X* was enough. Not technically a slave, she had a life sentence, nonetheless. Like the stories about the company stores in mining towns, the longer she worked the more in debt she became. Most contracts included extra "reasonable fees," penalties, handling cost, and sickness, including penalties for pregnancy and venereal disease.

There is an apocryphal story of Dah Pa Tsin, a successful madam on Church Alley. She was purported to have scores of women working in various brothels. She trained her employees to call or sing several English words, reportedly "date" or "China girl" to prospective American clients walking by crib windows. Thus, the name "sing-sing" became slang for a Chinese prostitute. In *À la California: Sketch in the Life in the Golden State*, we read a passage written by Col. Albert S. Evans as he strolled down the Barbary Coast. He observed that the girls had artificial flowers in their hair and painted lips: "Each colony [crib] of a half dozen girls was under the immediate control of an 'old mother,' herself a retired prostitute, who jealously watches over each, and receives from them the wages of their shame as fast as they are earned."

By the end of the century, the public outcry became too clamorous to ignore. Committees were formed and allegations were leveled. Some progress was made, but money changed hands, and the issue was whitewashed and facelifted. The 1906 earthquake and the ensuing fires burned Chinatown, putting an end to the sing-sing girls.

5

THE MOUNTAIN MEADOWS MASSACRE

ARKANSAS WAGON TRAIN MURDERED BY MORMON MILITIA

My conscience is clear before God and man. I am ready to meet my Redeemer.

—John D. Lee's last words before being executed

CEDAR CITY, UTAH TERRITORY, SEPTEMBER 1857

The US army was marching west to "annihilate the Mormons." Apostle George A. Smith was assigned by Brigham Young to tour southern Utah and have the Latter-day Saints prepare for war. Part of the preparation, Apostle Smith counseled, was to stockpile supplies. He also counseled them not to sell supplies to nonmembers. On September 7, 1857, the Fancher wagon train from Arkansas rolled into Cedar City (the southwest corner of Utah). The Latter-day Saints flatly refused to sell the goods the party needed to restock their wagons. The merchants were stiffly matter of fact, and the wagon train members were formally polite. Their journey through the territory had not been without incident, so the meeting was tense. A few drunken men harassed storekeepers, but Captain Fancher corrected them. Later, these men, further fueled by whiskey, found the Cedar City mayor's home and made rascals of themselves; their language was "colorful" and among their threats was "they'd be back with the US Army to help wipe out the settlement."

Photo just before the execution of John D. Lee for his role in the Mountain Meadows massacre, 1910. GIBBS, JOSIAH F. (1910) THE MOUNTAIN MEADOWS MASSACRE, SALT LAKE CITY: SALT LAKE TRIBUNE. OCLC 220893397.

Instead of prudently ignoring frustration and whiskey talk, the mayor and several church leaders took offense, wondering if they needed to make a show of force, some preemptive move to prevent retaliation. On Monday, September 7, 1857, several overly zealous leaders with a contingent of militiamen—without consent from church councils—decided to "sting" the Arkansas pioneers. Along with Paiute Indian allies, under the direction of John D. Lee, they dressed like Indians and attacked the wagon train. They ended up killing seven men and wounding sixteen others. What's more, they may have lost their anonymity. They feared that during a careless moment they could have been seen by several Arkansas men rounding up cattle. What had been an unauthorized "sting" would become a five-day siege.

In the current political climate, and considering what had happened, when local church leaders learned of the attack, they felt they had to cover it up with murder. It was a dark day for the Church of Jesus Christ of Latter-day Saints, informally known as Mormons. Local militia leaders from southwestern Utah set a deceptive trap. They planned to "destroy

John D. Lee, a Mormon who was executed in Utah in 1877.
UTAH STATE HISTORICAL SOCIETY.

everyone in the Fancher wagon train from Arkansas, except small children." The dead told no tales and thus blame would fall on the Paiute Indians.

Under a white flag of truce on Friday, September 11, 1857, John D. Lee, leading fifty or sixty Mormon militiamen of the Nauvoo Legion, rode toward the beleaguered Fancher wagon train from Arkansas. For five days these desperate men and women had fended off a deadly Indian attack. They viewed the Mormon militia as saviors. Captain Fancher had been killed and was buried in a shallow grave with the other dead. There were wounded who needed medical attention, and their water was nearly gone. Furthermore, they were so low on powder and ball, many had only one shot left.

Lee explained he was a government Indian farmer from Iron County and captain in the territorial militia. He told survivors he could guarantee their safety if they left their wagons and livestock and walked away unarmed. If they carried arms, he explained, the Paiute Indians would consider them "unfriendly" and attack. To ensure their safety, he said armed militiamen would walk beside them for protection. This was a bitter pill because the wagon train was composed of wealthy emigrants. They debated Lee's proposal and were naturally suspicious. However, the besieged men and women came to an inevitable conclusion: They had no other choice and must trust Captain Lee. They put their rifles in the wagons provided by the militia, covering them with bedding and a few other personal items. Curiously, Lee then divided the party into three groups. He explained this was for their protection. The smallest children and the wounded would go first, riding in the wagon. The women and children would follow. The men and older boys would take up the rear.

When the groups of emigrants were strung out along the trail, Major John B. Higbee stopped his horse and shouted, "Halt!" At his command, the militia were "to do their duty." The guards turned and shot point-blank while other militiamen and Paiute Indian allies stepped from their hiding places and fired. Samuel Pollock observed, "It sounded like one loud shot. It was perfect commotion." The Paiute Indians unleashed several fusillades of arrows and jumped into the fray. A man on the ridge said after the first volley, "A cloud of smoke hung over the valley," so he couldn't see what was happening. "The victims were butchered like hogs," said a man on the line. After the first shot, some of the men reloaded. Others followed up with bowie knives to save powder or "used the barrels and stocks of their rifles to finish off the women and children." Sam McMurdy, a teamster, said he heard a thud and turned to see the barrel of "a gun hitting the head" of a woman.

Nephi Johnson, watching from a hillside, reported, "most of the killing occurred in less than three minutes." Those who tried to escape were run down and killed by men on horses. But the bloodletting was not over. The militia still had work to do. There was no breeze, so a black powder smog clung to the ground, making the "cleanup" surreal. The soldiers were told to check each body to make sure the settlers were dead. A close-quarter killing field has a distinct odor. It smelled of rotten-egg sulfur, blown-out brain matter, and gut wounds commingled with the rusty scent of blood. Amid the "perfect commotion" of gore, there were the sounds of gunshots and the cries of surprise or pain coming from those not killed cleanly in the first rolling volley. And most haunting for many of the soldiers was the keening of a frantic toddler trying to locate a parent in the melee or the wailing sobs of a child hoping to bring a dead parent back to life.

One young soldier refused to kill a wounded woman. An older man named Stewards, frustrated by his lack of fortitude, demonstrated how it was done by burying his "bowie knife up to the hilt" in her body. He then took her children by the feet and "cracked their skulls over the wagon tires." Some reported sobs in the ranks. Conscientious objectors fired in the air or dropped to their knees. Captain Lee, a curious mix of Captain Ahab from *Moby-Dick* and abolitionist John Brown, called these men cowards. He said they didn't understand their duty as they were instruments in the hands of God.

Nephi Johnson said he tried to shut out the experience but failed. He *said* he didn't participate directly in the killing; however, he commanded a band of Paiute Indians and told them when to attack. Like all the men at Mountain Meadows, Nephi took a vow of silence—a vow he could not keep. After a long life without reconciliation, his deathbed words were "The Blood. The Blood." He has been compared to Kurtz from Conrad's novella *Heart of Darkness*. Kurtz's last words were "The horror. The horror." However, such a comparison is not entirely fair. Kurtz was a good man who chose the dark side. Nephi was a soldier in the territorial militia of the Nauvoo Legion who was drafted into action. He did not want to go.

A young boy watched his mother die and thought he was helping by pulling out the arrows sticking in her back. Another child was killed by the same bullet that killed his father. A six-year-old ran into the brush to hide and watched as her older sister was killed. When she rushed down to rescue her wounded baby sister, she had to untangle the child from her dead mother's bloody arms. That evening seventeen blood-soiled children, frightened and afraid, assumed to be too young to tell tales, were put into a wagon. "[They] arrived in the darkness of the night," said Rebecca Hamblin, a kindly ranch wife. She was worried about Sara Dunlap because a bullet had broken the bone in her arm. Rebecca knew the little girl would never use her arm and hoped it didn't get infected. Later the children were to be separated and adopted into Mormon families. After eating, Captain Lee wrapped up in his bedroll and went to sleep. He didn't hear that "the children cried all night," while Rebecca cared for them, comforted them, and treated their wounds.

The dead were hastily buried in shallow graves or thrown into gullies and covered with rocks and dirt so they would not be seen by another wagon train coming in a few days.

MOUNTAIN MEADOWS WAS A MASS MURDER

There is no polite way to say it. This was mass murder and an act of terror. The Mountain Meadows Massacre cannot be justified, condoned, or equivocated. Neither can it be mitigated, as it sometimes has been by good people in the Mormon culture who may not have all the facts or the emotional reservoirs needed to accept what happened. Mountain Meadows was the worst kind of behavior from the best kind of people. It must give us pause, and perhaps scare us, too; we must be wiser in an atmosphere of anxiety or fear.

A party of men, women, and children, mostly from Arkansas, lost their lives, their identity, and their story. They were the victims of treachery and deceit at the hands of "good" people who should have known better, a people who were, themselves, victims of mob violence. Almost 165 years later, the wound is still healing for some families in southern Utah and for the Church of Jesus Christ of Latter-day Saints. When I walk Mountain Meadows, I sometimes feel overwhelmed because this ground seems both haunted and holy, like Gettysburg, Normandy, or Dachau. Sometimes I've had to fight the nightmares that play in the back of my head because it seems too real. I want to yell "stop." As a historian I need to remain objective and keep to the facts, but as a human being this is difficult when a story, like this one, has personal roots. I am familiar with the names and biographies of the men, women, and children who lived and died here and have close friends who are directly related to the men who did the killing—neither they nor their families have ever forgotten. I appreciated their insight while preparing this chapter. Some of their stories—passed from generations to generation—are ugly. They have lived in a shadow, in a culture of shame. Some things I've not shared in this or other publications at their request. If you visit this historic site, don't be surprised to see flowers or messages that say, "We're sorry."

History is much more than facts, dates, and historical registers. It's about real people who didn't always make good choices and those who suffered as a result. There are complexities and stories that go beyond the kinds of cursory bullet points we had to memorize for high school or college exams. Rather, it's a study about journeys—a study about life. We will investigate two different groups, their cultures, their societies, their belief systems, and the problems they faced. Sometimes it's useful to think of the Latter-day Saints and the Fancher wagon train as independent moving parts that interacted. There is so much we don't know, but our understanding of this tragedy will be more complete if we look at it in historical context.

THE LATTER-DAY SAINTS MAKE A HOME IN THE WEST

In 1847, Brigham Young led the first wave of the Mormon migration across the Plains to the Salt Lake Valley, which was Mexican Territory. In 1849 after the Treaty of Guadalupe Hidalgo it became part of the United States. Young unsuccessfully petitioned to create the state of Deseret. As part of the Compromise of 1850, Utah became a territory and in 1851 President Millard Fillmore appointed Young governor. By this time, the Latter-day Saints were carving out new settlements and colonies in the Great Basin and southern Utah. It wasn't a Garden of Eden, particularly for farmers used to the Midwest, having some of the best farmland in the world. In this high, arid desert, even the weeds were sometimes strangled by the alkali soil. The Latter-day Saints hoped to settle unmolested and make a new life free from persecution. They had not forgotten the religious persecution they had faced and being driven from four states. Their beliefs, such as polygamy and their opposition to slavery, had fueled angry mobs in Missouri and Nauvoo. The famous trapper, Kit Carson, was so certain the Salt Lake Valley couldn't be farmed, he offered big money for the first bushels of grain. After the Latter-day Saints came West, Young applied himself to making the desert bloom. He didn't have a lot of patience with Washington bureaucrats who knew little about living on the frontier. He could be strong and opinionated, and his rhetoric was frequently fiery and hyperbolic. Like many Latter-day Saints, Young harbored a haunting resentment that the federal government had not done enough to protect their constitutional rights. This was the church's last stand, their stronghold, and they were not going to be driven away. This being said, he fiercely loved the United States and the Constitution.

It should be noted that territories didn't have the same freedoms the states had, which is the reason Young pushed for immediate statehood. Territorial leadership was chosen by the president who did not need to consider what frontier constituents were thinking. The marriage between the Latter-day Saints and Washington sometimes worked nicely; one example was the territorial supreme court, but overall, it was a marriage that required effort. All territories had growing pains, but few territories had the organic leadership that Young demonstrated. He didn't sit behind a desk; he was firmly at the front.

In fairness to the Latter-day Saints, not every appointee was a good fit. Some were openly antagonistic about it before they arrived in Utah. Others were antagonistic after they left. Some of the disaffected appointees were openly critical—especially in the press—suggesting that Young ran the territory like a tyrant. Later, this "bad press" would haunt the church, playing into President James Buchanan's plan.

Part of Young's plan was to establish colonies throughout the Great Basin and southern Utah. Such a colony was Cedar City, which was 250 miles from Salt Lake City. Cedar City was remote and isolated; there were no telegraph lines, and it was an eight- to ten-day roundtrip for an express rider. Young hoped to establish the Deseret Iron Company. Metals were a precious commodity that had to be shipped by wagon across the Plains. A foundry would reduce the cost of iron dramatically. The foundry, though, was never successful. It needed investment capital that was unavailable and was consistently on the verge of bankruptcy. The furnaces were makeshift and subpar, and unknown to the Latter-day Saints at the time the colony was established, the local coal contained too much sulfur to be effective. Cash was always in short supply. Most workers and suppliers were paid in credits at the company store. Ranching and agriculture were growing, but the members were quite poor. The Latter-day Saints in southern Utah were especially nervous during summer 1857 because they feared the Army would swing south, possibly wintering in Cedar City before going north to Salt Lake.

"BUCHANAN'S BLUNDER"

Democrat James Buchanan had been elected president of the United States when the nation was seriously divided over slavery. He was in a hot seat as he fought to keep the country from fracturing. He wanted time to put the pieces back together and try to mend the union. John Tyler, one of his advisors, sent him a letter with an idea that might give him and the nation some breathing room. Tyler suggested the Buchanan administration spearhead a plan to knock the haughty polygamist Mormons in Utah Territory down a few pegs. A further complication, Tyler noted, there was good reason to believe that Brigham Young and the Latter-day Saints were on the verge of rebellion. Such a move would not only divorce the Democrats from any association with Mormons, but more importantly, it would also divert the national attention from the slavery debate. Tyler wrote, "The popular idea is rapidly maturing that Mormonism . . . should be put down and utterly extirpated. I believe we can supersede the Negro-Mania with the almost universal excitement of an anti-Mormon crusade. Should you . . . seize this question with a strong, fearless and resolute hand, the country I am sure will rally."

President Buchanan created a large, costly problem out of a territorial scrabble. Sidestepping the real issue, the proverbial slavery elephant in the room, he made a "Mormon strawman" to divert the country's attention. He proclaimed the Latter-day Saints should "be put down and utterly exterminated." Under his direction, Colonel Albert Sydney Johnston led a contingent of twenty-five hundred soldiers west to take control of a "rebellious territory." Buchanan also replaced the territorial governor, Young, with Alfred Cummings. Such a move proved costly and ineffectual and was later referred to as "Buchanan's blunder." The Mormons, however, could see the persecutory cycle starting again. There had been territorial housekeeping details and disagreements between the settlers and the federal government, but the church considered themselves loyal Americans unless backed into a corner.

PREPARING FOR WAR

When the Mormon people heard that a large army under the command of Colonel Johnston was marching to Salt Lake City to "whip the Mormons," panic and fear ensued. Painful memories of the past persecution they had faced in the East resurfaced. The various branches of the Nauvoo Legion were called out for the "Big Fight." Young and church leaders advised the Latter-day Saints that war with the US army could be at hand.

Young knew the advancing army depended on having its supplies replenished when it arrived in Utah territory. It would be easier to starve an army than fight it. He told the Latter-day Saints he was prepared to "scorch the earth" if necessary, burning everything in the path of the approaching troops: buildings, fields, homes, businesses, and barns. The Mormons (along with their supplies and livestock) would retreat. As the Fancher wagons arrived in the Salt Lake Valley on August 3, 1857, the Latter-day Saints were taking the threat of the coming army seriously. Missionaries were called home to help defend their religion. On

August 2, Young mentioned the possibility of secession from the Union; the Church of Jesus Christ of Latter-day Saints would become an independent theocratic country. The next day, August 3, George A. Smith was sent to southern Utah, including Cedar City, to warn and prepare the people for war. On August 5, Young formally declared martial law.

THE FANCHER WAGON TRAIN

One company of settlers left Arkansas later in the season than was prudent. They planned to travel overland to California via Salt Lake City. They were led by Alexander Fancher and John Baker, both capable leaders. With more than forty wagons, carriages, horses, and hundreds of longhorn cattle, the overland trail took longer than expected. After crossing the Rockies, the party was understandably worried about making the Sierra Nevada Mountains before snow fell. It was the first of August before they reached the Salt Lake Valley. Some of the party wanted to make a risky dash, hoping to get over Donner Pass before the snow fell. It was the most direct route, but wiser minds prevailed. The Sierras could be unforgiving. Stories about the Donner party weighed heavily on their minds. A prudent course of action would be the southern route through the heart of the Great Basin and then across the Mojave Desert to Los Angeles. Captain Fancher was a good leader who had traveled this route before.

The Fancher Company had no idea they had stepped into a potential war zone. Normally, travelers planned to resupply at Salt Lake; it was considered the "Crossroads of the West." However, due to the church's recent moratorium on selling supplies to "gentiles," nonmembers of the Church, the company was not able to restock their wagons. On August 4 or 5, 140 settlers headed for Cedar City, 250 miles away. It was the only option. Frustrated by the timing, Captain Fancher felt there was a possibility to buy supplies in either Fillmore, Beaver, or Cedar City. They had money to pay for what they needed, but it was worthless if the Latter-day Saints weren't selling. Ordinarily, merchants would have welcomed the emigrants' gold; theirs was a cash-starved economy. Captain Fancher and his company ran into Jacob Hamblin and several Paiute Indians near a stream where both were camping and had a friendly exchange. Jacob told Captain Fancher that about thirty miles below his ranch, lay Mountain

Meadows, a good place to rest their livestock before the four-thousand-foot drop to the desert.

A WAR OF WORDS IN CEDAR CITY

On September 4, 1857, frustrated and disappointed the merchants wouldn't sell supplies, the Arkansas party started to leave. Several men who had too much Sagebrush whiskey, which they managed to buy in Cedar City, began to get abusive. Reportedly one man said, "If Ol' Brigham won't sell . . . we'll come back and take." Words from both sides were exchanged. Captain Fancher stepped in to censure some of his men. He realized that raised voices and angry exchanges wouldn't help. A bit later after the company had left, the men decided to visit the local mayor, Isaac Haight, informing him what they thought of Cedar City and the Mormons. They found his house and began shouting insults, hoping to get something started. Among the alleged insults were variations: "I have the gun that killed Joseph Smith." "We're going to come back to loot the town." "We're going to bring back some men and kill Mormons." "We're going to help the US army when they come and wipe you out." Haight slipped out the back door to find Sheriff John Higbee.

ISAAC HAIGHT PLANS REVENGE

Not only was Haight the Mayor of Cedar City, he was also the manager of the Deseret Iron Company, a stake president (a church leader), and a major in the local militia. Haight told Sheriff John B. Higbee to arrest the men for making threats, not keeping the peace, vulgarity, and public intoxication. The sheriff confronted the men, informing them they were not keeping the peace and that there were laws against vulgarity. The drunken men got pushy and dared Higbee to arrest them. Higbee, wisely, allowed the men to leave town. As they were leaving, according to lore, one of the men used a whip to snap the necks of several chickens. Another man verbally insulted several women. Both Haight and Higbee, as well as some of the citizens, were enraged and felt the Fancher party might need to be censured. Not only had Haight's honor been sullied, but they had also sullied the honor of the church. The two men felt they needed to enlist the militia to punish the wagon train.

Portrait of Isaac C. Haight. PUBLIC DOMAIN/WIKIMEDIA COMMONS.

To do this they needed to get permission from William Dame, the district militia commander. He lived in Parowan, a neighboring town about twenty miles away. Dame, also a stake president, understood the frustration. In his reply, he said to ignore them, "Words are but wind, they hurt no one."

By the next morning, Haight was getting angrier by the hour. Ignoring Dame's advice, he and several others considered sidestepping the militia. With several other town leaders, Haight came up with a plan. Why not have Indians attack the wagon company? He expressed his fear that unless these intruders were stung, they would come back raiding and killing. He knew the wagon train would rest for a few days at Mountain Meadows. The best place to have the Paiute Indians attack would be in a narrow gorge below Mountain Meadows. The track was steep, and the wagons would be spread out. To facilitate their plan, they needed the help of John D. Lee. He worked with the Paiute Indians as a federal Indian Agent and taught the local tribes how to farm.

Haight sent for Lee, who lived in Harmon, not far away. Meanwhile, Haight sent riders to follow the wagon train. By late afternoon Lee had arrived, and Haight explained, "Unless something is done to prevent it, the emigrants will carry out their threats and rob every one of the outlying settlements in the south." He also said one of the men had the gun that killed the prophet and maybe it was time to even up the score. Lee was certain he could enlist the Paiute Indians—especially if they offered the warriors the wagon train's horses and cattle. Haight made it clear the attack must occur in the gorge below Mountain Meadows when the wagons were strung out. Although the two talked all night, and Lee had a big breakfast before he left, Haight forgot to tell Lee the action was not approved by the district militia commander, Dame.

The next day, Sunday, September 6, 1857, Haight met with the Cedar City church council. He proposed his plan and argued that in the name of public safety, particularly with the US army coming to the territory, they must keep their settlements safe. The best solution was to have the Indians attack the wagons, so the Mormons didn't have a divided front. Again, Haight failed to tell the council he had sent Lee into action. Haight expected the council to accept his plan, but they did not. In fact, many had reservations and said he should send an express rider and seek advice from Brigham Young before they acted. In a huff, Haight stormed out of the meeting.

The next day, Monday, September 7, 1857, Haight got a message from Lee. Lee wrote that at dawn, the Paiute Indians had attacked the wagons. Sixteen members of the Fancher Party were wounded, and seven were killed. When Haight read the letter, he was livid. This was not what he had planned. He wrote to Young, reporting that the local Paiute Indians had attacked a wagon train. He also mentioned that members of the wagon train had threatened the Latter-day Saints in Cedar City; however, he left out the local involvement. He sent the note with an express rider, James Haslam, who would ride as rapidly as he could to Salt Lake. He then sent a letter to Lee telling him to "use your best endeavors" to prevent the Indians from any further assaults on the settlers. Lee would later explain that his plans were thwarted because the Indians botched the job. An accidental gunshot reportedly warned the trail-wise Fancher Company, and the Paiute Indians lost the advantage of surprise. What should have been a victorious dawn assault turned into a siege. The Indians had the wagon train pinned down, couldn't gain the upper hand, and were upset about their own dead and wounded.

THE SIEGE HAD BEGUN

Later that day, Haight received more bad news. Two members of the Fancher party had not been in camp when the dawn attack occurred. They had been rounding up cattle, and militiamen worried they might have been seen. They were able to kill one of the cowboys, but the other managed to return to the wagons. Over the next few days, Lee orchestrated more attacks on the wagons. On September 8, reinforcements were sent.

On September 9, Sheriff Higbee, who had been at Mountain Meadows, rode back and reported to Haight, telling him that the wagon train was running low on food and water. Because more wagon trains were expected, this complicated things. The two men decided they needed to call out the Mormon militia and kill all but the very young. They needed permission from William Dame, who still thought the Paiute Indians had attacked. Dame was considering sending in the Mormon militia to help the settlers. That night, Haight told Dame that the Latter-day Saints were the perpetrators and the Fancher Company knew it.

Accomplishing an extraordinary feat of riding, the express rider, James Haslam, rode into Salt Lake and gave the message to Brigham Young. In an hour, Haslam was back on the trail riding for Cedar City. Young's message for Haight was, "In regard to emigration trains passing through our settlements, we must not interfere with them until they are first notified to keep away." He also instructed. "You must not meddle with them. The Indians we expect will do as they please, but you should try and preserve good feelings with them."

On September 10, Haight met with Dame in the early morning. The Cedar City town bells rung to call up the militia. They rode to Jacob Hamblin's ranch. Hamblin was still in Salt Lake with the Paiute Indians. They met with Lee to decide the best way to kill the emigrants. At that point, many members of the militia assumed they were there to bury the dead. As the battle plan and the objective were explained, killing all but the very young, each member was sworn to secrecy. What they were doing was the will of God; they were protecting the Church. Many were disturbed about what they had to do, but they were living in a theocratic society and felt compelled to obey. (Theocracy, in a Latter-day Saint context in the 1850s was a fusion of traditional republican democratic principles—influenced by the US Constitution—where leaders are divinely inspired.) Their civic, church, and military leaders were often one and the same.

"TOO LATE, TOO LATE"

District militia commander Dame and Haight arrived at Mountain Meadows after the massacre. Severely affected at the sight of the dead children and women, Dame replied in a quivering voice, "I did not think there were so many of them, or I would not have had anything to with it."

6

THE MONTANA VIGILANTES

MONTANA GOLD MINERS TAKE THE LAW INTO THEIR HANDS

We the undersigned uniting ourselves in a party for the laudable pur-
pos [sic] of arresting thievs [sic] & murderers & recovering stollen
[sic] property do pledge ourselves upon our sacred honor each to all oth-
ers & solemnly swear that we will reveal no secrets, violate no laws
of right & never desert each other or our standard of justice so help us
God as witness our hand and seal this 23 of December.

From original signed oath document,
Montana Historical Society

BANNACK, MONTANA TERRITORY, 1863–1865

During the early days of the Montana Gold Rush, frontier justice was meted out quickly—often without due process. In all fairness, however, there was no law in the territory, and road agents were, excuse the pun, as thick as thieves.

In 1862, when gold was discovered on Grasshopper Creek in Bannack, Montana, men rushed to stake a claim. It produced $5 million in gold. All a prospector had to do was pull up a sagebrush bush and find gold by shaking out the roots. By 1864, about ten thousand men were seeking their fortunes. Southwestern Montana was an isolated location. The only way to get supplies or gold shipped out was on the Montana

Trail, a travel route between Virginia City and Salt Lake. It was a dangerous, lonely road. The weather could be brutal, Indian attacks were common, and outlaws found robbing easier than prospecting. One successful cartel of outlaws, ironically, was known as the Innocents, a shortened version of their password, "I am innocent." They preyed on travelers, stages, pack trains, and gold shipments. To combat these emboldened thieves, desperate miners and businessmen formed a group known as the Montana Vigilantes. The Montana Vigilantes fought lawlessness with their own brand of frontier law and order. Outlaws would be hung. Henry Plummer was a local tough guy who learned the hard way about crossing the vigilantes. In other parts of the West, Plummer had been an outlaw, a gambler, and a lawman, but he boasted that he could clean up the problem. He was appointed sheriff. There was a problem, though; Plummer was secretly an Innocent and was becoming rich tipping off his cronies about large gold shipments.

By chance, an outlaw named Erastus "Red" Yeager was caught. Before he had his neck stretched, he talked. Among others, he implicated Plummer. The Montana Vigilantes quickly put two and two together and realized their lawman was a serious problem. He had violated their trust and had robbed them. Over drinks, they discussed Plummer's fate. This was about as close to a trial as Plummer was going to get. On January 10, 1864, he was hung.

When territorial law was implemented, most of the Montana Vigilantes were happy to defer to an established legal structure. Many future Montana leaders were alumni of this group, including John Bozeman, a future US Senator; Thomas Dimsdale, the editor of the state's first newspaper; and Sidney Edgerton, the first governor, among others. In the nineteenth century, the term *vigilante* didn't have the pejorative meaning it does today. Even Theodore Roosevelt was a member of a vigilante group called the Stranglers.

Vigilantism can be a complicated discussion and is hotly debated. Some argue it is the forerunner of self-government, especially American self-government. Such "origin myths," according to historian Roxanne Dunbar-Ortiz, "form the vital core of a people's unifying identity and

Henry Plummer, sheriff of Bannack, Montana. PUBLIC DOMAIN.

value." Thus, taking the law into your own hands, often called "extralegal action," is part of our nation's cultural DNA. If there is no law or if the current legal system is ineffective when protecting a person's rights, you are justified taking the law into your own hands. On the frontier, especially during the early stages of boomtowns and gold rushes, there was no law. The problem is vigilantism can easily spin out of control. There's a danger in self-appointed, extralegal action, even when it appears to echo legal protocol. As we will see in the chapters of this book, extralegal actions can easily be hijacked by the opportunistic, the corrupt, or the misdirected.

MONTANA VIGILANTES

Mostly vigilantism in Montana didn't work because vigilantes swiftly became judge, jury, and executioner. When due process is not observed, innocent people get hung. In Bozeman, Montana, mob rule won. "Steamboat Bill" was a pimp. He threatened one of his Chinese prostitutes with a pistol. He needed fifty cents to buy cigars, and he thought she was holding out. His gun accidentally discharged, and he blew her brains out. He was waiting in jail until a circuit judge made his way to Bozeman. His plea was accidental death. Why would he kill a girl who was making him money? In jail with him was Z. A. Triplett. He came to town to drink whiskey, but he needed supper. He went to the restaurant and ate but refused to pay his bill. The owner physically threw him out, but not before he took his winter coat as collateral. He'd give the coat back when Tiplet paid the fifty cents he owed. After some drinks, Tiplet decided his honor had been violated. He went back to the restaurant and slipped his bowie knife into the man who wanted fifty cents. He was accused of murder and was also waiting for the circuit judge. Some local men were drinking, aware that the Bozeman City coffers were low. It was expensive to keep a couple of guilty murderers in jail incurring all that expense until the judge came. And who knew when that would be? The men would likely hang. To save the city of Bozeman the jail and hanging expense, they could do the hanging themselves. They used a log to break down the door of the jail, and a couple of men distracted the sheriff by putting a pistol in his face. The vigilantes then hung the two men.

STOPPING THE INNOCENTS

In 1863, there was a string of robberies that indicated an inside man. The robberies were too well-planned.

- October, a merchant was robbed. The outlaws took $12,000 in gold dust.
- October, a stage was robbed near Bannack. The outlaws took $2,800 in gold.
- November, a man was robbed. The man thought he had Henry.

Painting by John W. Norton of Henry Plummer's gang holding up and robbing a stagecoach (1863).

HOUGH, EMERSON (1907) *THE STORY OF THE OUTLAW: A STUDY OF THE WESTERN DESPERADO*, THE OUTING PUBLISHING COMPANY, NEW YORK.

- November, a stage was robbed. The road agents likely got about $1,000.
- December, a stage was robbed and the robbers got about $1,500.
- December, a stage was robbed of $81,500 of gold and notes.

While the Montana Vigilantes had suspected Sheriff Plummer, they didn't hang him on the spot. They wanted tangible proof. Erastus was going to hang. He wasn't getting a deal, the confession and indictment of Plummer was enough. On January 10, 1864, the day he was taken into custody, he was hung.

7

A WICKED TOWN AT TRAIL'S END

THE MYTHIC VERSUS REAL DODGE CITY, KANSAS

[Ed Masterson] was not large, but there are not few men who would be anxious to tackle him a second time.

—*Dodge City Times*

DODGE CITY, KANSAS, LATE IN THE 1870S–1880S

In Dodge City, Kansas, real men died from bullets fired from real guns. Gunfights in the West, however, almost never looked like a staged Hollywood scene in which two men postured face-to-face, abruptly drawing their shooting irons to see who was fast enough to win the deadly contest. Neither was it akin to a jousting tournament in which two noble knights spurred their horses at the drop of a flag, charging boldly to lance his opponent. Eastern newspapers didn't get it right either with sensational headlines such as, "Vigilantes Amusing Themselves . . . Sixteen Bodies to Start a Graveyard at Dodge City." In the thick of the wild days of Dodge City, a period of approximately twelve years, there were fifteen documented murders, not fifteen per shoot-out. In the real Dodge City—unlike its exaggerated image—the dead were not stacked like cordwood before being taken to Boot Hill. For those who were killed, yes, it was the most lethal town on Earth, but mostly Dodge was much like other cow towns.

Gunfights were not pretty. They often occurred like the following account of the death of town marshal Ed Masterson. A hundred miles

Front Street, Dodge City, Kansas, 1874, with Robert Wright and Charles Rath's general store, Chalk Beeson's Long Branch, George M. Hoover's liquor and cigar store, and Frederick Zimmermann's gun and hardware store.
PUBLIC DOMAIN/WIKIMEDIA COMMONS.

north of Dodge City, foreman Alf Walker hired six cowboys to help with the spring roundup in the Smokey Hills. Walker wanted to gather in the strays before the herds arrived from Texas. When their work was done, Walker and his cowboys went to Dodge City for a few days on the town. At the Lady Gay, one of Walker's cowhands, Jack Wagner, was wearing his gun, which was forbidden in city limits. Walker and his cowboys were thoroughly liquored up when Masterson and a policeman named Nat Haywood noticed Wagner was armed. Masterson quickly disarmed Wagner, giving his pistol to either the barman or to Walker; accounts differ. Either way, Masterson left firm instructions that Wagner was not to get his weapon back until he left town. Masterson had done this hundreds of times. Men often forgot to check in their guns, eager for a night on the town; nevertheless, Masterson was hired to keep the peace, and he did his duty.

Masterson and Haywood exited the saloon and were lingering outside, talking to friends, and enjoying the evening. After a while, Walker walked out of the Lady Gay. He was followed by Wagner who was wearing a gun again. Maybe he borrowed a revolver from a friend or the barkeeper—or Walker returned his gun. We don't know for sure. Either way, Wagner was armed. Masterson moved quickly to disarm Wagner again and was direct.

This time there were angry words. Reportedly, Wagner's friends stepped in as either Wagner was drawing his gun and Masterson moved to check and control the weapon, or Masterson was reaching to disarm Wagner. Wagner saw what Masterson was doing, and he tried to get his gun first. Whatever happened, it occurred very fast . . . maybe in two-tenths of a second. Walker, presumably to help Wagner, had now drawn a weapon, and then there were shots. An observer said they sounded like a burst from a Gatling gun—the number is a matter of debate—but there were five bullet wounds and likely stray shots that fortunately went wild. Three men were shot, and two would die. The other shooter was most likely Bat Masterson, the sheriff of Ford County. He arrived too late to save his brother but got a bullet in each of the cowboys.

Deconstructing a gunfight is not simple. Forensic experts have differing opinions. The gunfight at the O.K. Corral lasted thirty seconds, and the Masterson shooting was a couple seconds at most. Walker reportedly shoved his pistol in the face of Dodge City policeman, Nat Haywood. Others said Walker pulled the trigger, but the hammer fell on a bad round

Interior of the Long Branch Saloon in Dodge City, Kansas.
PUBLIC DOMAIN/WIKIMEDIA COMMONS.

or an unloaded cylinder. We aren't certain, but we do know Haywood had the hell scared out of him and ran away in fear. He would later resign from the police force. Wagner took a slug in the abdomen and died painfully the next day. Walker took a bullet in the lung and two in the arm. The doctor thought he was going to die, and the first few weeks were horrific. His recovery was long and grueling, but he surprised everyone and lived to a ripe old age. Until his passing Walker would carry a bullet doctors couldn't remove. Ed Masterson was shot in the side and reportedly managed to walk to the bar in a saloon. He had not noticed his clothing was smoldering because he'd been shot at point-blank range. He's supposed to have said to the bartender, "George, I've been shot." He died within the hour.

THE LEGENDARY DODGE

A mythic Dodge City, Kansas, both feared and loved, fascinated the public's attention. Newspapers, magazines, and pulp fiction fed readers' seemingly unquenchable appetite for story after story about the West's most iconic town. One headline read, "Three Men Bored with Bullets and Thrown into the Street." Readers learned of fabled gunmen who were lightning fast on the draw, of perilous outlaws who haunted the dangerous streets of Dodge, of unflinching lawmen who brought them to justice, of two desperate men meeting on the dusty main street at noon, and the sinful dens of iniquity. Typical of the headlines of the day or the multicolumn article in the *New York Tribune*, one article was headlined, "The Diversions of Dodge City." It was critically stated that in, "Dodge City there is no law. . . . There are no sheriffs and no constables." The assumption was killers and miscreants did as they pleased. Consequently, headlines about lethal happenings in Dodge echoed the make-believe West, "Terrible Times on the Border. How Things Are Done Out West."

Because Dodge was a notable town, its roll read like an Old West *Who's Who*. Besides the Masterson Brothers, Ed and Bat, the town hosted their brother Frank Masterson, and Bat's friend, a former buffalo hunting partner, Wyatt Earp. Among the others the town hosted were Luke Short, Doc Holliday, Bass Reeves, Clay Allison, and Elizabeth "Libby" Thompson, aka Squirrel Tooth Alice.

A REPUTATION WAS SPUN

By the 1860s, steam-driven mills could make inexpensive paper from the wood pulp, providing inexpensive paper not only for newspapers but also for publications known as "the pulps." These included often mass-produced news sheets, tabloids, and magazines, as well as novels, among other kinds of books. They were cheaply printed and inexpensive, appealing to a mass readership. The pulps also opened a thriving new market for advertising. Selling copy, increasing circulation, and maintaining a loyal readership was their business model.

In the nineteenth century, newspapers didn't necessarily feel obligated to report objectively many had a defined political bias. Communication systems were primitive and fact-checking was not an art form. Much that was printed was boilerplate from other papers; but this was the mass media of the day. Tabloids and magazines were popular and gave rise to what was called "sensational" or "yellow journalism." It would be characterized by eye-grabbing headlines and exaggerated story details meant to excite the readers. Such articles used what facts and details they could find, or glean from other articles, and rewrote them. Comparably, it would be similar to a high school student who can write a clean seventy-five-word essay but needs to turn it into three-hundred-word essay because that's the required assignment. Dodge City earned some of its reputation honestly, but a good portion was spun by sensational writers who would receive high marks for their creative writing. Dodge City was also closer to eastern publishers than most frontier towns, and wire service and rail lines were quite accessible. It was cheaper to send a reporter to Dodge City than to Denver or San Francisco. Getting the latest scoop on what was happening in Dodge and getting it out was nineteenth-century real time. Even the uptown publications got into the act.

Of course, no one did more to put Dodge in the public eye than Harry Gryden. Gryden was a Swedish immigrant who became a lawyer and moved to Dodge in 1876. Opening a law practice, he loved what's called the "sporting" life: gambling, drinking, and sporting events such as boxing. He was friends with both Wyatt Earp and Bat Masterson. He realized he was sitting on a "journalistic" gold mine as he was rubbing shoulders with some of the most famous men on the frontier. He began writing immensely popular pieces for the *National Police Gazette*. To say his pieces were sensational would be damning with faint praise. True, he was living in Dodge and had an inside track—unlike the other writers—but he didn't want to limit himself. If it was a slow day, he could invent a scenario with his characters. The *Gazette* was an incredibly popular publication; so much so, it was called "The Barbershop Bible."

THE DODGE CITY OF HISTORICAL FACT

Adhering to western standards for a cattle hub, Dodge City was about average. Local merchants needed the cowboys' business, but they didn't think highly of the herders' reckless and wild behavior after a long trail drive, which was known as "cutting the wolf loose." Local vigilantes and "bought lawmen," known as the Dodge City Gang, worked at keeping a tentative peace. In the name of public safety, the gang became the enforcement, if not the quasi-legal tool of the business interests.

The real Dodge was a dangerous town because it was on the frontier. It had been a buffalo and a rail town before it was a cow town. It had a business district, mercantile operations, banking, outfitting, supplying, and shipping, and there was the vice district. After a town was established, there was an understood border if not an actual border that separated the two. The vice district was considerably "dodgier" than the business district, and there were places inside the vice district that were universally menacing. When there were a lot of young, single men who did dangerous work and carried guns and knives crowded into compact areas drinking a lot of alcohol, there were going to be differences of opinion. As the saying went, "dangerous pleasures for dangerous men who live dangerous lives."

The Dodge City Gang did not always represent the community. Wyatt Earp, Bat Masterson, Luke Short, and Bill Tilghman, among other famous bully boys, knew who signed their paychecks, and they protected their employers, as well as their own shady business interests, with badge and Colt. They habitually bent or broke as many laws as they upheld.

THE HISTORY OF DODGE CITY

In 1871 a rancher built a three-room sod cabin five miles from Fort Dodge and opened a trading post. It would become Dodge City, Kansas. It was near the Santa Fe Trail and the Cimarron cutoff. By 1882, it would be known as the buffalo-hunting capital of the world. The Atchison, Topeka, and Santa Fe railways had arrived, so Dodge became an important depot. The town was filled with buffalo hunters, railroad workers, soldiers, and travelers. By1873, to keep order businessmen formed the Dodge City Peace Commission. Dodge City was no longer safe for families, businessmen, or their clients. True the town made its living selling supplies, but it also made a great deal of money promoting diversions for men who wanted to visit the saloons, dance halls, gambling halls, and brothels. The Peace Commission hired Billy Brooks as the quasi-lawman to help keep the peace. He was supposed to be a gunfighter but was a disappointment.

Dodge City Peace Commission, early in June 1883. The men went to Dodge City armed to support Luke Short in a confrontation with business interests that wanted to force him out of town. The title of "peace commission" (later applied to the photo) was ironic. Their presence did not produce a peaceful resolution. According to a biography of Wyatt Earp by Casey Tefertiller, the photo was taken in the Conkling Studio at Dodge City in June 1883 and first appeared in the National Police Gazette on July 21, 1883. From left to right, standing: W. H. Harris, Luke Short, Bat Masterson, W. F. Petillon. Seated: Charlie Bassett, Wyatt Earp, Frank McLain (possibly "M. C. Clark"), and Neal Brown.
PUBLIC DOMAIN/WIKIMEDIA COMMONS.

Law Enforcement Officers

Law enforcement names are inherently unclear because they are used interchangeably by the public, in newspaper articles, and in legal documents. Proper use is confusing. For example, a deputy could be a deputy US marshal or a deputy sheriff. A marshal could be US marshal, a deputy US marshal, a city marshal, or a deputy city marshal. At times, any law enforcement officer was called a sheriff. A detective might be referred to as a marshal or a sheriff, a brand inspector, a hide inspector . . . or a private detective, for example a Pinkerton or Wells Fargo agent. To make things more perplexing, it was possible for a lawman to represent two or three different agencies simultaneously. Double- or triple-dipping was not considered improper, because officers were generally not paid well. A town marshal or deputy could be a commissioned deputy US marshal and a Pinkerton detective—or any combination—in the same town. But there are specific differences.

Federal Officers

US federal marshal. Appointed by the president. Their purview was enforcement of federal or territorial laws. These officers were spread over large regions.

Deputy US marshal. Appointed by the marshal, as needed, or budget allowed. These appointments were often temporary, supplying needed help for the marshal.

Indian police. American Indians recruited from a specific tribe or group of tribes. They worked under the direction of the marshal or deputy.

State Officers

Ranger. These were state police, enforcing state laws and protecting citizens. The most famous are the Texas Rangers. In the early days of Texas history, the Rangers brought in their fair share of outlaws, but their primary job was fighting Indians and keeping the frontier safe.

Brand/Hide inspector. Usually a state job, but an inspector could also be a county employee.

County Officers

Sheriff. A county law enforcement official elected by popular vote. Some of the sheriff's jobs were enforcement of county laws, tax collection, and keeping peace in the county.

Deputy sheriff. Appointed by the sheriff, deputies did much of the day-to-day law enforcement.

Constable. Often a deputy town marshal or sheriff.

City or Town Officers

Town marshal. Appointed by the town municipality to enforce city laws, keep the peace, and clean manure off the city streets. Responsible for handling the drunk and disorderly. The town marshal's jurisdiction ended at the city limits.

Town deputy marshal. Appointed by the town marshal.

Private Law Enforcement Officers

Private detective
Pinkerton Agency
Wells Fargo
Stock detective

He wasn't up to the job—nor would he be the last marshal in Dodge City to either be run out of town with his law enforcement tail between his legs or to take a bullet. In 1874, to show the committee meant business, the commission decided they could take care of the problem themselves. They sent six offending ringleaders a "get out of town or else" notice. Four of the six wisely left. The commission theoretically knew what to do and loaded their shotguns with buckshot. As the story goes, one of the offenders didn't die like he was supposed to, so a commission member walked over to the wounded man and put a bullet in his head. This killing was problematic because the man worked at Fort Dodge. The army received special permission to arrest the Peace Commission, and one of the members was brought to trial. By the next year, a reorganized municipality decided to lay down a few actual rules. Because railroad tracks already split the town, they created what they called "the Deadline." The north side of town would be where legitimate business would be transacted. The south side would be the bawdy houses, the beer and whiskey joints, and the gambling parlors. They passed a law that firearms would not be allowed but must be checked in on North Front Street. By 1876 the buffalo were nearly gone, but the new gold was cattle. During November 1877, the assistant town marshal, Ed Masterson was keeping the peace at Bar's Lone Star Dancehall. Reportedly Wyatt Earp was in the saloon when a couple of questionable characters wearing sidearms entered, shooting the sheriff and scaring off two deputies in the process. Earp, who was just passing through, mentioned to the mayor this was no way to run a town and that these men needed someone to stand up to them. The mayor is said to have taken the badge off the body of the sheriff and handed it to Earp, saying "You're the sheriff."

8

THE TEXAS TIN HAT BRIGADE

MAYBE THE BLOODIEST VIGILANTE GROUP IN THE WEST

When it is understood that the honest, legitimate citizens were in the minority and scattered over a large area . . . the necessity to organize a Vigilance Committee to rid the community of these lawless characters when the law was impotent . . . becomes apparent.
—Edgar Rye, Shackelford County, Precinct Justice

FORT GRIFFIN, TEXAS, 1874–1878

The vigilantes called themselves the Tin Hat Brigade. They were proud of their handiwork; they sometimes kept score. When a horse thief named Houston Fought was lynched, the Tin Hats pinned a sign to his swinging corpse, "Horse Thief no 5." As an afterthought someone scratched, "Shall Horse Thieves Rule the County? He Will Have Company." Fort Griffin prided itself on being one of the "wickedest" cities in the West. It was known as the frontier Babylon on the Brazos—hosting all the sinful pleasures of the flesh. Itinerant preachers compared it to the iniquitous "cities of the plain" in the Old Testament.

Indulging in the seven deadly sins was understandable. Breaking the Eighth Commandment, however, "Thou shalt not steal," could bring swift retaliation. Offenders, were lynched. The Tin Hat Brigade could historically be footnoted as one of the most lynch-happy groups of vigilantes in the West. Rumor has it they strung up more than two dozen men. In one famous anecdote, a horse thief was lynched from a shade tree in the middle of town. It seemed no one bothered to cut him down. A pick and shovel lay on the ground beneath him, along with a sign hastily scribbled and pinned on the condemned man's shirt read, "Bury him if you feel the need." Folklore says he hung for three months. His decaying body was a callous object lesson.

The editor of the newspaper the *Frontier Echo* supported this kind of frontier justice, "The gang of horse and cattle thieves which have infested Shackleford County . . . have received a death blow." In other editions, he touted additional approval, "Yesterday, his body was hanging to a tree three miles from here." The editorial also said that the vigilantes left a sign with a skull and crossbones as a reminder. In another headline, "Two *men* were dangling in the air." Later, the editor of the *Frontier Echo* remarked that thus far "the vigilantes had not made a mistake."

However, such frontier justice could spin out of control, and it did. Especially, when a local crime boss, a vigilante member named Jim Larn, got elected sheriff and met his fate. Even the famous gunfighting gambler, Doc Holliday, in an apocryphal tale spun by Wyatt Earp, barely avoided the hangman's noose. If it wasn't for the quick thinking of his girlfriend, the prostitute Big Nose Kate, Holliday would have swung.

In the 1860s, West Texas was arguably "the most dangerous prairie" on the frontier. In 1867, the army built Fort Griffin on the bluff above the Clear Fork of the Brazos River. The town of Fort Griffin, located below the bluff, was born. The town was sometimes referred to as "the Flat" or "the Bottom." It became a boomtown because it was a natural crossroads, supplying southern buffalo hunters, cattle drives, ranchers, and the US cavalry. It was the last stop on the western trail for anyone going north to Dodge City, Kansas, or going to El Paso. There was always the ever-present threat from raiding Comanche and Kiowa Indians, as well as lawless white men who lived by plunder and murder.

The clientele were mostly young, single men with money to burn. Purveyors of all vices gathered like moths to a lantern. Fort Griffin would host many legendary Western characters, including gamblers such as Doc

"Big Nose" Kate Horony. PUBLIC DOMAIN/WIKIMEDIA COMMONS.

Holliday and Lottie Deno; famous prostitutes, such as Katie Elder and Big Nose Kate; and gunmen such as Pat Garrett, John Wesley Hardin, John Selman, Wyatt Earp, and Bat Masterson.

FORMING THE TIN HAT BRIGADE

Characteristic of many boomtowns, growth outpaced the legal system. Extralegal order, vigilantism, filled the vacuum. Sometimes it was better than nothing, but at best it was flawed. Even when there were frontier municipalities, towns and counties were poor, and it took money to build a jail or a courthouse, hire lawmen, judges, and prosecutors. In 1874, the town was so lawless, the US army was forced to impose martial law.

Because business in a boomtown was speculative, entrepreneurs were reluctant to invest in infrastructure or municipal luxuries. They had come to Fort Griffin for one reason: to ride the wave, make money as fast as they could, and get out if the town faltered. They weren't harboring dreams about building to last or doing community service. Such entrepreneurs didn't want the army or law enforcement meddling in their affairs. It seemed that the Tin Hat Brigade formed a practical, effective method for protecting their business interests and investments. They felt they were capable of handling their own brand of self-government. Besides, why wait for a jury's inevitable "guilty" verdict? There were plenty of trees and everyone had a length of rope. Furthermore, when law and order did raise its head, it proved to be ineffective. As the town grew and seemed to be more stable, businessmen were a frustrated by a sophomoric legal system that couldn't get a conviction.

JOHN LARN ELECTED SHERIFF

In 1874 a likable man named John Larn joined the Tin Hat Brigade. He saw it as a business opportunity. The town may have been unaware of his past or didn't care. Larn had killed a rancher in Colorado and was rumored to have shot a lawman in New Mexico Territory. By 1873 allegations had surfaced that on a cattle drive from Texas to Trinidad, he had murdered several Mexican herders. Nevertheless, he was popular and elected sheriff. He said the right words and appeared to be an ideal choice for a lawman.

As the new sheriff, though, he showed his true colors by hiring a hard case named John Selman as his deputy. Selman was as corrupt as his boss and would go down in history as the man who murdered the gunman John Wesley Hardin in a saloon. He shot Hardin in the back of the head while Hardin was playing dice. Larn and Selman made an intimidating team and were adept at manipulating the system for their own coffers. They brokered stolen cattle and secured profitable beef contracts with the army, among other illegal ventures. As sheriff, Larn manipulated the vigilantes into acting as his personal band of enforcers, reducing competition and masking his own criminal activities. Sinister tales have circulated about the two lawmen. One has them lynching a man they said was a rustler and appropriating his cattle.

As their crooked business ventures became apparent, complaints became prevalent. Larn resigned as sheriff but pulled strings to get himself appointed as the county hide inspector. It was his job to inspect all the hides leaving the county, making certain brands hadn't been altered and the sales were legal. It was also his duty to inspect butchering operations. He was hired to help prevent rustling, but this appointment only made it easier for him to move stolen cattle. His flagrant activities caught up with him when ranchers complained about lost cattle. A search warrant was issued in winter 1878. Illegal hides were found in his possession, so he was arrested. He was soon released, but his dirty deals had made him a number of enemies, including influential members of the Tin Hat Brigade.

On June 28, 1878, Sheriff William Cruger served another warrant for Larn's arrest. Fearing that Larn's friends might try and break him out of jail, Sheriff Cruger chained him to the floor of his cell. By now, the ex-sheriff had further incurred the enmity of the Tin Hat Brigade. In the eyes of vigilantes, he had violated their trust and was a bona-fide cattle thief. There was also speculation that he knew too much about the vigilantes. Either way, he needed to be lynched, so the Tin Hat Brigade broke into the jail to string him up, but there was a problem. They couldn't pick the locks on his chains. Hanging was obviously their first choice, but a firing squad would do. They blasted the two-timing sheriff with six shooters, rifles, and shotguns. Now that they were warmed up, it made sense to do a little more housekeeping, so they also hung a suspected rustler from a tree near the river. Coincidentally, a local marshal named William Gilson, rumored to have been in league with some rustlers, also disappeared that night.

DOC HOLLIDAY

A town this wicked attracted the likes of Doctor John "Doc" Holliday. Holliday had a table at John Shanssey's Saloon. In fact, it was in Shanssey's that Doc met his on-and-off lady friend, Mary Katherine Horony, known as Big Nose Kate, and Wyatt Earp. Holliday liked gambling at Shanssey's. For the most part, it was a safe place to gamble. Shanssey had been a prizefighter and no one wanted to cross him. Earp rode into Fort Griffin as a deputy US marshal. He had been trailing a man named Rudabaugh who was wanted for a robbery. Knowing about Holliday's reputation, he asked Shanssey, "He's a killer, isn't he?" Shanssey replied, "He's killed some but not around here."

One night, Holliday was playing poker with a man named Ed Bailey. Despite Shanssey's rule about not causing trouble, Bailey, they said, was looking for trouble. During the game, he began to look at discarded cards, which a player wasn't supposed to do; it's called "deadwooding" and is considered cheating. Holliday reportedly warned him several times. Bailey did it again, so Holliday swept the pot and the game was over. This wasn't a whimsical reaction on Holliday's part, but a standard house rule. Bailey took offense and went for his gun. Holliday reached for his bowie knife, which was handy. With an orchestrated swipe, he effectively gutted Bailey before he could clear leather. Holliday had a proven record with both weapons. According to Earp, Holliday had what we'd call a "situational awareness." It was a critical life skill for a sickly gambler with tuberculosis.

Cheating while gambling was considered a serious offense. However, calling someone out or implying they were cheating, even if they were, was a violation of the code. Defending your good name was obligatory, especially if you were on the prod. Bailey went for his gun, so Holliday used deadly force—a justifiable homicide in the West. Of course, Holliday, who must have read "tells" rather well, must have known that taking the pot was the same thing as calling Bailey out.

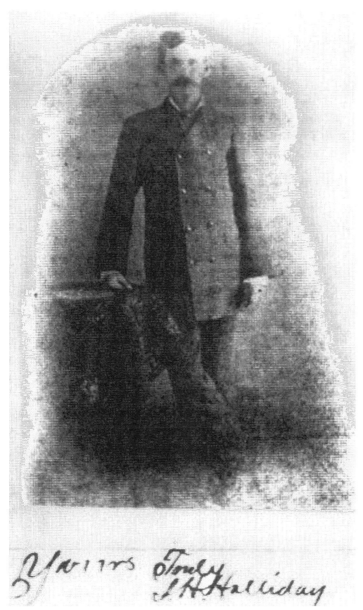

This is a copy of a photograph of Doc Holliday taken by an unattributed photographer in 1879 in Prescott, Arizona.
PUBLIC DOMAIN/WIKIMEDIA COMMONS.

In his day, though, there was little question he'd be cleared as soon as the sheriff investigated. He willingly submitted to what was a technicality in a Western town, self-defense. Surely, if Holliday felt there was going to be a problem, he would have left Fort Griffin on a fast horse. Trying to do things legally, it seems neither he nor the sheriff considered the mood of the crowd. Almost immediately, according to Earp, vigilantes gathered, like flies at a picnic. Maybe they were some of Bailey's friends or, perhaps, the local mob fuel by drink wanted to teach this gambler a lesson. As Earp suggested, "Doc's life wasn't worth a plug nickel." He had surrendered his weapons and was taken into custody. As we've learned, jails at Fort Griffin are not vigilante proof. Considering the mood of the town, the sheriff thought Holliday would be safer if he stayed in his hotel room, a couple of deputies stationed nearby. Apparently, they were not just to prevent his escape but to provide protection from the mob. It also appears that Holliday and Kate had more than a business relationship. Kate could read a crowd and knew she needed to save the man she loved. (Holliday, incidentally, once commented that she was his intellectual equal, even if she was a whore.) So she moved quickly. The clever Kate borrowed a second Colt revolver because she had one for herself. Packing her things and lining up a few saddle horses, she created a diversion by setting a barn on fire; fire was a serious threat. Even vigilantes understood their first civic duty was firefighting. Dressed in men's clothes, the wily Kate freed Holliday. The two star-crossed lovers rode their stolen horses four hundred miles to Dodge City, Kansas, aiming to begin a new life together.

In vigilante culture, this story is important, and so is the subtext. The message is even a tough gunman like Doc Holliday can get caught in a mob maelstrom. There is one important caveat about the Holliday and Kate story: It's probably not true. Earp seems to be as truthful as the storytelling Odysseus in the *Odyssey*. Nevertheless, with that said, this vignette has been retold, so often its nearly sacred in the Holliday canon. However, scholars have serious questions about its authenticity. There are no documents or extant newspaper accounts that corroborate the critical details. For example, who was the man Holliday reportedly killed? There was no record of his name. Was the name Ed Bailey made up to make the story more realistic? Frankly, the first we hear about Bailey is

Unconfirmed photo of Doc Holliday.
PUBLIC DOMAIN/WIKIMEDIA COMMONS.

in an article in *San Francisco Inquirer* years after Holliday's death. Then the name resurfaces again in Stuart Lake's 1931 biography, *Wyatt Earp: Frontier Marshal* (a fun read but slenderly factual).

The colorful Earp was not a historian; rather, he was promoting Wyatt Earp. Earp lived until 1929. Part of his livelihood was being a living Western legend playing, well, Wyatt Earp. He was a consultant for an exciting new genre, the Western cinema, and exercised a significant influence on a brilliant young director, John Ford. Ford would go on to make some of the greatest Westerns of all time. As a point of interest for students of the American West, when we read quotes from Wyatt Earp, think of Mark Twain's *Huckleberry Finn*, "he told the truth, mainly. There are things he stretched."

9

LOS ANGELES VIGILANTES MASSACRE CHINESE

NINETEEN MEN HANGED IN RACIAL ATTACK

[The Chinese are] directly responsible for this blighting vice. . . . and at their door must it be laid with a thousand other mortal sins.
Reno Evening Gazette, February 21, 1879

LOS ANGELES, CALIFORNIA, 1871

Word spread throughout Los Angeles. "Calle de los Negros" was in a state of revolt. Chinese men were killing Los Angeles citizens. A policeman and a rancher had been murdered—maybe more were dead. Several tongs had been fighting each other but set aside their differences and were shooting Americans. Anglo and Hispanic citizens rushed side by side to protect their city. Five hundred vigilantes had gathered to see justice done. Anti-Chinese feelings that had been festering now burst into violent action. The Los Angeles vigilantes were not only putting down a riot, but they were also taking a stand on a moral issue. The so-called Celestials were a threat to American decency and values, if not an outright evil. A recent cartoon in the 1869 *Harper's Weekly* summed it up. The picture showed a Chinese man holding a white woman. The caption said something about the Pacific Railroad was now complete.

The lawmen were doing their job, but chaos and disorder were everywhere as the citizens stepped in to help. Some of the vigilantes were commissioned by law enforcement to guard a building where suspected tong members had taken refuge. They were to prevent anyone from escaping. Ah Wing, a tong gangster, had been captured. He had in his possession a four-barrel weapon—one of the barrels had been discharged. Somehow Wing escaped from his guard but was recaptured. He had a hatchet in his hand, a favorite tong weapon, so he was shot by a policeman. Another man burst out of a building and was repeatedly shot. If suspected Chinese terrorists were in a building, the vigilantes used axes or picks to make holes in the roof so they could shoot at movement below. In three different locations, Chinese men had been shot and strung up. One hanged man had his forefinger cut off, so a looter could take his ring. His pants were also taken, apparently to search for valuables. When Los Angeles Chinatown was under control, nineteen Chinese men were summarily hanged. Many had a number of bullet wounds. This was visual evidence, in case someone needed reminding, who was in control.

A fight among Tong members triggered a vigilante retaliation, but many of the men were looking for an excuse. At the time of the massacre, the population of Los Angeles was approximately seven thousand. There were around two hundred Chinese. The majority were men, and most of the women were prostitutes. The number of Chinese immigrants in California was increasing. The growth in Los Angeles and surrounding towns was no exception. Whites resented their presence, feeling that Asians took jobs, as many politicians and labor leaders were suggesting. Hostility was growing, fueled by a surging national spirit of nativism, which was fostered by newspapers and magazines. Moral crusaders were suggesting that the damned Chinese were eroding American values. Because of their close proximity, their licentious nature would be corrupting. An example was the young white boys who would surely be seduced by Chinese women. Even the San Francisco police chief had written in his report to the state he had seen white women and Chinese men side by side in opium parlors. Because of the inherently lecherous nature of Chinese women, a virulent venereal disease would become a physical threat.

Los Angeles Chinatown was located on a street called Calle de los Negros, or alley of black people. It was named by the European colonists

This photograph shows corpses of Chinese immigrants who were murdered during the Chinese Massacre of 1871 in Los Angeles, California.
LOS ANGELES PUBLIC LIBRARY, SECURITY PACIFIC NATIONAL BANK COLLECTION.

from Spain. This street was where those of mixed, darker blood, dwelt— American Indian, African, and Spanish mixed breeds. By the time the first migrations occurred, the street was quite run down, but it was affordable. At best, it was a rough, crowded neighborhood. Multiple dwellings and businesses were jammed together: brothels, cribs, opium dens, bars, and gambling parlors, as well as eating places, laundry services, and shops.

FEUDING TONGS

Tongs were generally careful about keeping their affairs inside Chinatown, but their feuding had begun to cross racial lines. Tong conflicts were common enough, but they became public news when someone outside the Chinese community got hurt. Previously, two rival tong members had shot at each other and missed. They were released on bail, but such activity focused attention on tong disputes, especially when firearms were used. The skirmish that triggered the violence was over a woman. More specifically, it was a fight about to whom she belonged. Most Chinese women were prostitutes, virtual slaves, and considered a valuable property to their owner but also a property worth stealing. To get around US laws, by 1870 most Chinese women had to be "married." This was a business formality so a woman could get past inspectors.

In the past if a tong member abducted a prostitute from another tong, a reward would be posted. Local law enforcement would help recover the woman and receive a finders' fee. This practice kept tongs from directly fighting one another and was good for the community and lawmen. On one occasion, though, it didn't turn out well because two lawmen got into a fight. Joseph Dye, a constable, was angry with the town marshal, William Warren. They were both looking for a prostitute who had been kidnapped and taken fifty miles away to Ventura. Constable Dye wired the local marshal and asked him to hold the prostitute until he could pick her up and bring her back to Los Angeles. However, Marshal Warren was already en route and got to Ventura first. Warren took custody of her and received the finder's fee. When Dye met Warren, he had his derringer hidden in his hand. They argued, Dye fired and missed. Both men pulled their service pistols and shot. Warren missed, but Dye did not. He shot Warren in the groin. He died of his wounds.

On October 23, 1871, two tongs were battling over a prostitute named Yit Ho. A Los Angeles officer named Jesús Birderrain was killed, along with Robert Thompson, a local rancher, who attempted to intervene. News of the murders ignited the city, fueling the vigilantes, which resulted in the massacre.

After the smoke cleared, ten white vigilantes were arrested, but only eight were tried for their part in the murders. They were convicted of manslaughter and sentenced from two to nine years in San Quentin. An appeal was submitted to the state supreme court. They overturned the conviction, sending the case back to Cameron Thorn, the Los Angeles district attorney. Thorn decided not to retry the cases. Animosity still existed in Chinatown, and he wasn't sure he could get a conviction.

THE "CHINESE QUESTION"

The "Chinese Question" became so important, it was an issue in the presidential debate in 1876. Although there had always been racial tension, it began drawing national attention. In 1876 and into the 1880s persecution became more pronounced. Many laws were passed depriving Chinese of even marginal civil rights, such as the right to own property. By 1880, arguably 76,000 Chinese immigrants lived in California. In other states there were 9,500 in Oregon; 3,250 in Washington; 5,400 in Nevada; 3,400 in Idaho; 1,600 in Arizona; 914 in Wyoming; 500 in Utah; and 57 in New Mexico. Stereotyping and racial slurs continued. As a result of the hostility, The Chinese Exclusion Act of 1882 reduced the flow of "cheap Chinese labor" to the United States. Wages had not increased and thus created a form of economic slavery. The street Calle de los Negros became Los Angeles Street in 1888. The Geary Act was passed in 1892, restricting entry into the United States. Chinese immigrants who were in the United States prior to the passage of the law were required to carry resident permits on their person.

10

BILLY THE KID AND THE LINCOLN COUNTY WAR

THE REGULATORS FIGHT "THE HOUSE" IN A RANGE WAR NOBODY WON

I'm not afraid to die like a man fighting, but I would not like to be killed like a dog unarmed
Billy the Kid in a letter to Governor Lew Wallace, 1879

LINCOLN COUNTY, NEW MEXICO TERRITORY, 1878

John Tunstall had come to the United States to make his fortune. He knew his ranch on the Rio Feliz was no longer safe. His business partner, a lawyer named Alexander McSween, refused to release insurance money from a trust account to their arch business rival, James Dolan. McSween said he needed to look at Dolan's financial records so he could substantiate Dolan's claim through the probate court. Dolan refused. McSween, knowing Dolan desperately needed the $7,148, used every legal trick he could manufacture to get continuances.

Frustrated, Dolan charged McSween with embezzlement. Dolan was a powerful man in Lincoln County, the head of a business organization called the "House." Dolan asked a judge on his payroll to seize McSween's assets. This was economic combat, so Dolan took a step further and had the judge issue a writ against Tunstall's property, too.

It was no secret that the Lincoln County Sheriff, William Brady, was in league with Dolan. Tunstall learned that Sheriff Brady had deputized a posse of outlaw gunmen to seize his property. They'd start with his herd of horses. Tunstall wasn't ready for a direct confrontation, but he refused to capitulate. He felt he'd be safer in Lincoln, thirty miles away. Through his foreman, Dick Brewer, he hired several known gunmen as ranch hand/bodyguards, including Billy the Kid. After breakfast, Tunstall and his party headed for Lincoln. Later, when the sheriff's posse arrived at Tunstall's deserted ranch, Deputy Buck Morton, the leader of the posse, knew if they rode hard, they might catch Tunstall before he got to town. Among his riders were a number of well-known outlaws Dolan and the House used for rustling cattle, including Jesse Evans and his "Boys."

By afternoon, the Tunstall party had made good time. They had taken a mountain shortcut. Spread along a narrow mountain trail in the late afternoon, some of the men veered off the path to bag a few turkeys for dinner. Billy the Kid was riding drag when he saw the posse coming up fast, so he warned the others. A rider named Middleton, who was close to Tunstall, tried to get the Englishman to follow him. Apparently, Tunstall didn't understand or wasn't aware of the danger. The posse had started shooting, so Tunstall's riders were exposed on the ridge and were forced to take cover. Several of the posse, including Buck Morton, Jesse Evans, and Tom Hill, saw that Tunstall was still on the trail below them.

This was better than they could have expected; it was almost too easy. In the scrub brush, out of sight from the others, they swooped down on him like a pack of wolves cornering a fawn. Their orders were to murder him "resisting a lawful order." Deputy Morton would later say that Tunstall went for his pistol, so it was self-defense. They caught up with him and quickly put a bullet in Tunstall's chest. And for good measure, they put another bullet in his brain.

As if to tag their work, they shot his horse in the head and, reportedly, positioned Tunstall's body, hat on his head, so he looked like he was sleeping next to his mount. Meanwhile, Tunstall's men were still pinned down, but they said they could hear the shots. Then there was a long

The only surviving authenticated portrait of Billy the Kid. Retouched and restored by Mmxx. PUBLIC DOMAIN/WIKIMEDIA COMMONS.

hesitation, and two quick pistol reports. The assumption was the killers fired two rounds from the dead man's handgun to bolster their claim of self-defense. The House had drawn first blood. The Lincoln County War had begun.

There would be no heroes. Justice would not be served. Neither side would have a clear victory. For many, especially the smaller ranchers and farmers, their distrust and resentment lingered for years. The war emphasized that justice was, indeed, blind because the law could be bought, used, and manipulated by the wealthy or the legal practitioners who knew every jot and tittle.

Folklore, fiction, and films might have the luxury of painting the Lincoln County portrait as black and white—making the players on the canvas good or bad. In the factual historical narrative, however, it's never that simple. Both sides in this war were corrupt. Maybe a better question would be to ask, "which side was less corrupt?" In the 1870s, Lincoln County was much larger than it is today. In fact, it was the largest county in the United States, roughly the size of South Carolina. In this arena, two factions, two rings of economic bullies, fought for a monopoly, proving they'd do anything to succeed. Violence and intimidation were tools, just as the system was a tool. As in most feudal confrontations, it was dangerous to remain neutral.

Not unexpectedly, this range war morphed into a larger-than-life spectacle. Even in its own day, it earned national, if not worldwide headlines. It was the press's version of a Wild West Show—not the news. It was entertaining drama. There was romance, shoot-outs, hoofs and horns, rustling, gunfights, revenge, gunslingers, Billy the Kid, mean land pirates, open ranges, and the US army riding in to save the day.

This chapter will explore the Lincoln County War and its most famous personality, Billy the Kid, and how he weaves in and out of this narrative. It's important to understand what was happening in New Mexico Territory in the 1870s—the Santa Fe Ring and the "land grabber." Then we'll look in more detail at Lincoln County and the rivalry that led to the bloody conflict between the House and the Regulators.

THE SANTA FE RING AND THE NEW MEXICO "LAND GRAB"

Unfortunately, all the press fanfare overshadowed other issues: corruption in the territorial and federal bureaucracies, land fraud, and racial tensions. The New Mexico Territory had the largest nonwhite population in the Union, which largely outnumbered the white settlers. Because of the peonage tradition in New Mexico, even though the "Peon Law" was passed in 1867, it was possible for a small minority of reconstructionist "land grabbers" to displace Hispanic populations, thus garnering vast tracts of land and creating a disproportionate prosperity. The Hispanic populations, like the American Indians, had no political voice. Such actions created a different kind of tenant bondage that was a form of economic slavery.

Several of the key players, called the Santa Fe Ring, included territorial governor Samuel Axtell; Attorney General, Tomas Catron; and Judge William Logan Rynerson. The Ring had long fingers stretching throughout the territory, including railroads, mining, government contracts, and resource development. One of their specialties was restructuring Spanish land grants so they could "legally" take control of the land. One case in point was the eviction of Hispanic "squatters" from the Maxwell land grant. For the Santa Fe Ring, quasi-legal framework, land speculation, and fraudulent land deeds were a thriving opportunity—not unlike organized crime. Front men, such as Lincoln County's Lawrence Murphy, James Dolan, and John Riley, did a lot of the Ring's dirty work; they were enforcers, franchise enforcers. Payola was the model. Thomas Catron, a principal in the Santa Fe Ring, was also principal investor for the House. Catron came to the territory in 1866 and was an important member of the New Mexico territorial system. He served as district attorney, attorney general, and US senator. Catron owned three million acres of land, making him one of the largest private landowners in our history, and had a county named after him, even though he was involved in the infamous Teapot Dome Scandal during Warren Harding's administration.

The New Mexico political machine had become so corrupt that the territory would not achieve statehood until 1912. For example, in 1900 President Theodore Roosevelt did his best to clean out the state's corruption, firing two territorial governors. Trying to right the wrongs, he said to

George Curry, "All I ask of you is that you give an absolutely honest and common-sense administration." Almost as a frustrated postscript, Teddy wrote, "I am quite at a loss to know how to discriminate between those who are decent and those who are not."

CORRUPTION IN LINCOLN COUNTY

Before the Lincoln County War turned bloody, it was ugly. After the Civil War, New Mexico Territory was a wild and perilous land, but it was also a land of promise for those willing to fight Comanches and Apache Indians, brave the elements, and displace the American Indian and Mexican populations. To make the land theirs, the developers and settlers had to "take and hold" before they sculpted and fashioned farms, ranches, or businesses. As we've learned, the Lincoln County War was a battle between two entrepreneurial forces: the House and the Regulators. The House was getting rich on a crooked monopoly it had created. The Regulators wanted to get rich by taking the crooked monopoly away from the House. What happened was a no-holds-barred fight: bribery, double dealing, intrigue, political machinations, election manipulation, fraud, intimidation, robbery, and murder. They say twenty-some people died (surely the number was higher because Hispanics were rarely included in white body counts or those shot and never found).

To better understand what happened between February 18, 1878, when John Tunstall was murdered, and the five-day shoot-out, from July 15 to 19, 1878, known as the Battle of Lincoln, let's look at the perilous state of affairs that ignited the final act. Some have called this feud a five-month war, but such a label is too tidy. The bitterness and the complications lingered for years.

The House

Lawrence "L. G." Murphy came to the New Mexico Territory in 1869. At Fort Stanton, ten miles from Lincoln, he started L. G. Murphy & Company. With business partner Emil Fritz, they operated a brewery and a store. However, they specialized in selling land they didn't legally own—as well as carrying the mortgages. If payments were late, they gladly foreclosed, assuming the crops and livestock. In 1873, Fritz was diagnosed with a serious illness, so he sold his share of the business to James Dolan, who was the bookkeeper. When Dolan tried to shoot an army captain, Dolan and Murphy were asked to leave Fort Stanton. They relocated to Lincoln, ten miles away. They needed to be close because they had large beef contracts with the army. In the meanwhile, Murphy's former business partner, Fritz, had gone to Germany, his homeland, and died. He left a $10,000 life insurance policy that Murphy felt should go to him for some of Fritz's "unspecified" outstanding business debts. This policy would soon become a serious point of contention.

In Lincoln, Dolan and Murphy constructed a new building for their store and business headquarters. It looked like a large house, thus the "House." William Brady, a Dolan and Murphy crony, had moved to Lincoln and was elected sheriff in 1870, giving the House an added advantage. When Murphy was diagnosed with bowel cancer, Dolan would take over the day-to-day operation of the business. At this point, they'd added John Riley as a partner. Riley was a good friend of the cattle-rustling element in the county. At this time, Murphy sold his "share" of Fritz's life insurance policy to Dolan. Sheriff Brady had become executor of the Fritz estate.

The Regulators

The faction opposing the House called themselves the Regulators. In that day a regulator was a vigilante group that fought corruption, especially "legal corruption." The key players were John Chisum, cattle baron; Alexander McSween, attorney; and rancher/entrepreneur John Tunstall. Using Tunstall's business model, these men saw an economic opportunity and took it. Chisum funded the plan but had little personal involvement. McSween arrived in 1876 and quickly became disillusioned with Murphy. With the help of his new associates, they opened a rival mercantile in Lincoln. They charged fair prices and drew many customers away from the House. McSween wasn't above using shyster lawyer schemes that profited him. He wasn't prone to physical violence, but he played hardball with his business deals and preferred to fight in court. The Regulators hoped to buy grain and cattle from local farmers and ranchers at a better price than the House offered. Sheriff Brady made little progress on

Fritz's insurance policy, so McSween was hired by the Fritz family. He knew how to process the claim with the New York insurance company. He got the money, but he put it in a trust account and threw legal hurdles at Dolan; specifically, he wanted to see what Fritz's debts to Dolan were. This intensified the rivalry. McSween knew that the House store was near insolvency, and he didn't want them to have a cash infusion.

In August 1876, Tunstall arrived with an ambitious plan to become wealthy and "run the county" in three years. Unlike the movies and fictional accounts, Tunstall was not an older gentleman from Scotland with blue blood. He was born in London. His father was a successful middle-class merchant. The twenty-four-year-old Englishman was surely scrappy, if not always wise. Tunstall could turn on his charm and sell his dreams with enthusiasm, but his letters home show he was also prepared to be a coldhearted businessman. Using people, in his mind, was good business. His charm was one of his tools. He wrote to his father that he planned to get half the money in the county. He started by buying a ranch on the Rio Feliz, about thirty miles south of Lincoln. He named his business J. H. Tunstall & Co.

BILLY THE KID

The most eclipsing character, of course, in this Old West morality play was Billy the Kid. He's arguably the most popular "gunfighter," if not one of the most famous characters, in Western history. He could be charming and witty. He's been vilified and glorified. It seems he's been elevated to a naughty-boy rock-star status. There are more than fifty movies about him. The first was a silent film, *Billy the Kid*, in 1911. On August 28, 2021, the Colt .44-40 Pat Garrett used to kill Billy the Kid sold for $6 million. However, in any sort of final reckoning, we must remember, superstar status or not, he was a murderer.

Officially, Billy the Kid's name was William Henry McCarty. He was also called Henry Antrim because in 1873, his mother married William "Uncle Bill" Antrim. To avoid the "William" confusions, she called him by his middle name, Henry. Later, he adopted the alias, William H. Bonney. He was called Billy, of course, from William. We're not sure about Bonney. It might have been a family name or part of his natural father's name. He was young and diminutive, so he was often called "Kid" or "the Kid"—sometimes "Kid Antrim." By 1880 the press had settled on the headline-grabbing "Billy the Kid."

McCarty was born September 17, 1859, to Irish immigrants living in New York City. His mother was Catherine, and we think his father's name was Michael McCarty. Some of the details are a little cloudy because there is no verifiable marriage certificate. Catherine was widowed but quite determined; as a single mother she fought her way out of the abysmal Irish ghetto and took her family West. Catherine proved to be a good businesswoman, owning a laundry service. There are ads for the City Laundry in a Wichita, Kansas, paper. She prospered enough to buy 160 acres and made certain her sons were educated. Tony Connor, one of Billy's friends, said, "Billy got to be a reader. He would scarcely have his dishes washed until he would be sprawled out somewhere reading a book." He loved adventure stories. He could certainly write, and we can see this in his letters.

In June 1871, Catherine received bad news. She was diagnosed with tuberculosis. She liquidated her Wichita assets and moved to a drier climate. Her boyfriend, Henry Antrim, followed her to Denver and then to Santa Fe, where they were married in 1873. In March of that year, they relocated to Silver City about ninety miles away. The boys liked their "Uncle Bill" who treated them kindly. Antrim prospected and did odd jobs, and Catherine worked until she was too weak and bedridden. She died on September 16, 1874. The boys' stepfather stayed for a little while, that is, until the lure of new goldfields was too strong, and they were orphaned.

From September 1874 to September 1875, Billy worked at a butcher shop for room and board. He was involved in a local theater—discovering he had a flair for acting, singing, and dancing at the opera house. Without his mother's guiding hand, he would soon be involved in petty crimes, like stealing butter. Louis Abraham, a friend, commented, "He was a good kid, but he got in the wrong company." A fifteen-year-old Billy and an older friend, who wanted to be called "Sombrero Jack" (George Shaffer), broke into a laundry. The *Grant County Herald* of September 26, 1875, said Billy "was charged with stealing clothes from Charley Sun and Sam

Chugs [laundry]." Billy took the bundle and hid, apparently not carefully, because he was caught red-handed by his landlady, who called the sheriff. Knowing his situation, the lawman tried to scare the lad straight. The newspaper article said that Billy "escaped from prison . . . yesterday through the chimney."

From September 1875 until August 1878, Billy was in Arizona—scared but not straight. He fled to Arizona. For the next two years, he frequented the area around Camp Grant (about seventy miles east of Tucson). He worked on a ranch learning something about the cowboy trade but reportedly he was fired because he was small. The foreman thought he was not physically able to do heavy ranch work. This was likely a bitter pill, but he did learn something from the cowboys; he was introduced to firearms and the finer points of shooting. By 1876, sixteen-year-old Billy had done some rustling, but his specialty was stealing saddle blankets and saddles from army horses tied to the hitching rail while the soldiers were drinking at the saloon. He got bold and took a soldier's horse but was caught. Billy was locked up, escaped, and then got caught again. The second time he escaped in shackles from the guardhouse.

The next summer, in August 1877, a "made over" Billy resurfaced at Camp Grant. He walked into George Atkins Saloon, no longer a slipshod waif. Instead, he was dressed more like a foppish toff, wearing fancy store-bought pants and shoes, not boots. He must have looked out of place in a frontier saloon. Perhaps it was his inner thespian—life was a stage—manifesting itself. There was nothing dandy, however, about the Colt comfortably shoved in his waistband. A blacksmith who worked at Camp Grant, Francis Cahill, was said to be a bit of a bully. There are several variations of this story, but they all end with a bullet. Cahill teased Billy and said he looked like a pimp and even roughed up his hair. He may have slapped and pushed Billy down. It got heated and "you son of bitch" flew through the air. Billy's honor had been besmirched. Like Mark Twain's character Tom Sawyer, Billy had read the romance literature, or something akin to it in dime novels and the *Police* Gazette: A man must protect his honor. Also entrenched in the "cowboy code" and embarrassed in front of all the men in the saloon, he had no choice. He went for his Colt and shot Cahill in the stomach. Cahill would die the next day.

According to folklore, Billy was lightning with his draw. But in this fight, he wasn't that fast because Cahill saw that Billy was drawing and caught the gun, trying to wrest it from his hand when the pistol went off. A coroners' jury decided the sixteen-year-old should be held for a grand jury to see if a crime was committed. Frightened, Billy didn't hang around for the inquest and got the hell out of Camp Grant. Billy turned his back on Arizona and rode for Lincoln County, New Mexico Territory.

By late in September 1877, William Bonney was riding with a band of serious outlaws, the infamous Jess Evans and the "Boys." He had crossed a dangerous line; he had killed his first man. He was about to step into one of messiest range wars in history.

HIRING GUNMEN

Battle lines had been drawn. The House threatened legal action as it flexed its economic and political muscle. Reportedly, Dolan challenged Tunstall, to a duel. Tunstall is supposed to have said something like "I hire others to do my fighting for me."

The House rogues' gallery of Southwestern outlaws was already in place, including Jesse Evans and his "Boys," the John Kinney Gang, and Seven Rivers Riders. They had rustled for the House and shared a mutual antipathy for John Chisum. Evans had worked for Chisum in 1872. Chisum had hired Evans to make raids on the Apache Indian reservation to steal their horses. By 1875, Evans had gone out on his own. Evans had also worked for John Kinney, and the two were good friends and business associates. Kinney's ranch was an ideal place to collect stolen cattle, which Kinney would wholesale to John Riley. Riley also rode and did business with another group of rustlers called the Seven Rivers Riders. They were a cantankerous bunch from the Seven Rivers Valley. The Seven Rivers Riders were ranchers with small enterprises who had been at odds with the ever-expanding Chisum operation.

Tunstall knew he needed gunmen, too. But he had no idea what he was up against. Certainly, Chisum had plenty of riders, but he was keeping a low profile. Fortunately, Dick Brewer, who had a ranch next to Tunstall's and worked as Tunstall's foreman, was helpful. He knew ranchers and cowboys who were sympathetic to the Regulators. But they were getting a late start. Brewer hired cowhand gunmen, including a teenager who'd been in a few scrapes with the law. Brewer quite liked Billy. Besides, Billy had quit riding with "the Boys." In the folklore, we often hear that Tunstall became the father Billy never had and they were close. This certainly makes a nice story, but it's not accurate. Tunstall treated Billy well, and Billy clearly liked and respected his employer. Tunstall bought him a new rifle. It's obvious that Billy appreciated Tunstall's sense of order and purpose and looked up to him. To imply a filial bond between them is bending a thin branch too far. Tunstall was only twenty-six years old. Also, records show Tunstall didn't spend much time at the ranch. Billy was hired before Christmas 1877 and Tunstall was murdered in February 1878.

During the Lincoln County War, there were forty or fifty men who rode with the Regulators, including many Hispanic vaqueros.

JOHN TUNSTALL'S MURDER

Looking at the murder of John Tunstall, the riders who were with him on that fateful February day were Dick Brewer, Billy the Kid, John Middleton, Henry Newton Brown, Robert A. Widenmann, and Fred Waite.

The day after the murder, Billy the Kid and Brewer swore affidavits to the justice of the peace, John Wilson, and were deputized. Billy was shaken and said, "They killed Mr. Tunstall. They shot him down like a dog. He's in the Sanchez Canyon." The men knew it was Billy's job to protect Tunstall, and they'd let him down. At this point, Sheriff Brady stepped in, took their weapons, and threw them in jail. Because they were locked up, they missed John Tunstall's funeral. Billy's anger and rage escalated.

While I'm speculating, it's possible to hypothesize that this was a turning point in his life. No longer a self-centered kid-drifter, Billy had a reason to stand up and be counted. Shooting Cahill in the bar was about his personal honor. While he vowed revenge, it was more than personal. He felt a sense of justice and balancing on a larger moral scale. It's obvious that he considered himself a soldier. Whatever Tunstall's inner, aloof feelings might have been for his employees, Tunstall had given Billy what every eighteen-year-old wants most, a "man's respect." Tunstall had not ruffled his hair or teased him. Tunstall had treated the teenager like an adult; he'd given Billy a brand-new rifle. And, so he sat, jailed while the murderers were running free. He was incensed by the hypocrisy and corruption that he had witnessed, and he lost faith in the system of justice—a system whose loyalties went to the highest bidder. Justice was something that he would administer with a Colt pistol and a Winchester rifle.

BLACK WATER CREEK MURDERS

Finally, with arrest warrants, the posse set out to bring in Tunstall's murderers on March 1, 1878. Some of the riders were Billy, Dick Brewer, Frank McNab, Doc Scurlock, Jim French, John Middleton, Frank Coe, Jose Chavez y Chavez, Charlie Bowdre, Tom O'Folliard, Fred Waite, and Henry Newton Brown.

Near Black Water creek on March 6, 1878, there was a running gun battle. Finally, Buck Morton, who was the head of the House posse, and Frank Baker agreed to surrender to the Regulator posse leader, Dick Brewer, if he'd guarantee their safety. Fearing the two men would be freed and overriding Brewer, the posse decided to fill Morton and Baker with many slugs. William McCloskey was also shot.

Three days later, on March 9, the House pulled in political favors. The territorial governor, Samuel Axtell, "reversed" Justice Wilson. This meant that Governor Axtell decreed that the Regulator posse was formed illegally. Justice Wilson had no legal right to deputize the men. Thus, the Regulators had acted illegally and were guilty of murder. Sheriff Brady had murder warrants for the Regulators.

SHERIFF BRADY IS SHOT

On the morning of April 1, six of the Regulators, including Billy the Kid, positioned themselves by a corral. When Sheriff Brady and deputies walked up the street, the Regulators opened fire. Brady was shot more than a dozen times. Billy and Jim French foolishly ran to Brady's body. According to legend, Brady was using the rifle Tunstall had given Billy, and he wanted it back. Both Billy and Jim French were slightly wounded. The Regulators felt they had administered justice. In the eyes of the community, they stepped over the line. Because Billy would become famous, he was also credited with a number of shootings he may not have committed.

AN OVERVIEW OF THE LINCOLN COUNTY WAR

It was called the Battle of Blazer Mill. The Regulators found Buckshot Roberts and there was a gun battle on April 4. Buckshot Roberts and Dick Brewer were killed. Billy was grazed by a bullet. George Cole had a finger shot off, but John Middleton was seriously wounded with a bullet in his chest.

Many of the Regulators, including Billy, were formally indicted for the murder of Sheriff Brady about two week later on April 18.

In a gunfight called the Ambush at Fritz Springs, the Seven Rivers Riders wounded Ab Saunders, and Frank McNab was killed on April 29. Frank Coe was taken prisoner.

The next day in Lincoln, a Seven Rivers Rider was wounded, and several others were killed. About two weeks later on May 15, another Seven Rivers Rider was killed.

The Battle of Lincoln, which was the largest gunfight in the Lincoln County War, began on July 15 and went on for five days. The Regulators were holed up at McSween's house and store, and the House gunmen and Seven Rivers Riders shot it out for days. The numbers of dead and wounded varied, but the Regulators lost at least five men and the House lost two men. The US army was called in to support the House. On the last evening, Mrs. McSween and the children were allowed to leave the McSween home, and then the house was set on fire. McSween was killed and several of the House gunmen were killed. The rest of the Regulators escaped in the confusion.

WHAT TO DO WITH LINCOLN COUNTY?

A few murders had occurred, and the town was in a state of shock. President Rutherford B. Hayes said, "The main street in Lincoln is the most dangerous street in America." Governor Axtell had replaced Lew Wallace. The county was considered so dangerous warrants were not served, district court was postponed, and no one wanted to serve on a jury. On November 13, 1878, Governor Wallace declared an amnesty for Lincoln County—if there were no prior indictments. Having had former indictments, Billy the Kid would not be eligible. James Dolan was taking steps to get Tunstall's ranch

Alexander McSween's widow, Susan McSween, hired Huston Chapman as her attorney. On February 18, 1879, Chapman was murdered. Dolan was suspected but would not face charges. Dolan bought Tunstall's ranch. Rustling continued in Lincoln County. In 1880, a politically ambitious Pat Garrett was elected sheriff by a narrow margin. He was voted in on a law-and-order ticket and supported by John Chisum. Billy the Kid came to represent all that was wrong in Lincoln County, and Garrett vowed to bring him in.

ON THE RUN

After spending some time dodging deputies and bounty hunters, Billy realized the futility of the fight and hoped it could go away. A new territorial governor was appointed, as well as a federal investigator. Billy had asked for amnesty and was willing to testify against Dolan who murdered Chapman. On March 18, 1879, Governor Wallace was to meet with Billy secretly. The two ostensibly agreed to a "deal." Billy surrendered to the sheriff on March 21, 1879. He testified; however, the district attorney wouldn't let Billy go nor did he grant Billy amnesty. Angered, Billy broke out of the Lincoln County jail on June 17, 1879 but continued to press the governor through letters arguing his case. He managed to stay out of trouble for a time, but on January 10, 1880, Billy killed a man in Fort Sumner. Governor Wallace offered a $500 reward. On December 23, 1880, Garrett, the law-and-order sheriff, killed several Regulators and captured Billy at Stinking Springs. Billy was returned to jail. He was tried in Mesilla, New Mexico, and found guilty of murdering Sheriff Brady. On April 13, 1881, he was sentenced to hang. According to legend, the judge supposedly told Billy he would hang until he was "dead, dead, dead." And Billy reportedly said, "And you can go to hell, hell, hell."

THE LAST ESCAPE

Sheriff Garrett, being a cautious man by nature, quickly took Billy to the blacksmith's and had his arms and legs shackled. Bob Olinger and James Bell were assigned to guard him because Billy had a way of vanishing. Garrett and Billy knew each other but were never close friends. Garrett was civil and polite, but Olinger was reported to have been abusive.

Portrait of Sheriff Pat Garrett. PUBLIC DOMAIN/WIKIMEDIA COMMONS.

The guards had been warned to be careful, but as history proved, they didn't take their jobs seriously enough. Olinger bragged, "Billy has no more chance of escaping than he does of going to heaven." They apparently didn't know the Kid's hands were smaller than his wrists. Garrett was gone, so the time was right for Billy to escape.

On April 28, 1881, Olinger was at dinner. Billy asked Bell to take him to the privy. When they were out of sight, Billy slipped the cuff off one wrist and swung the chain and the empty cuff as hard as he could at Bell's head. The man went down, but he wasn't out. The two fought for Bell's pistol. Billy claimed he didn't want to hurt the jailer, but the man kept coming at him, so he shot him. He went to the office to get the key to unlock his leg irons. After freeing himself, he grabbed Olinger's shotgun in the corner of the room. When Olinger returned, Billy shot him with both barrels and made his escape.

PAT GARRETT KILLS BILLY THE KID

Billy the Kid's escape was an embarrassment for the sheriff, who vowed to hunt Billy down . . . again. A new $500 bounty was issued. Garrett was relentless. After four months of searching, Garrett sat in a dark room waiting on July 14, 1881. He heard Billy's voice, and Billy came in the room. Garrett wasn't going to take any chances, so he shot at what he thought was Billy. His first bullet hit Billy's heart. His second shot missed. No one has said how long it took the outlaw to die.

Garrett was interested in collecting the bounty and restoring his name. Hoping to capitalize on his fame, Garrett, with ghostwriter Marshall Upson, published *The Authentic Life of Billy the Kid*. Garrett added a bit of gore for his audience. He had killed Billy after all, so it was only right that he got in on the act. His book didn't sell well because it wasn't authentic.

11

ELLEN "CATTLE KATE" WATSON

HUNG BY WYOMING RANCHERS WHO WANTED HER LAND

She had to be killed for the good of the country.
—Charles Penrose, *The Rustler Business*

SWEETWATER RIVER, WYOMING TERRITORY, 1889

Ellen Watson has the dubious honor of being the only woman hung in Wyoming. It took a moment to get the ropes over the stout branch before the nooses were uncomfortably settled over the heads of Ella Watson and her husband Jim Averell. Without ceremony, rancher John Bothwell shoved Watson off the lip of a rock. Someone else pushed Jim. The six ranchers watched as the couple suffocated. Each time Watson or Averell gulped for a panicked fraction of a breath, the hemp rope tightened as if it were a large constricting snake with prey in its coils. Both kicked hopelessly in what was called the death jig. Averell grabbed for the rope above his head but couldn't get enough purchase to lift himself up. Because the ropes were too close together on the branch and the victims' hands and feet had not been tied, each displayed spasms of hysteric terror as they tried to climb up each other for relief. At one point it was like watching a drowning woman trying to get a drink of air as she desperately clutched, shinnied, and pushed down the man who could not save her. In her last convulsions, Watson kicked off her buckskin moccasins, and blood came out of her mouth. The tongues of both victims swelled to exaggerated proportions as they twisted. The six ranchers were not experienced executioners, so they had not planned carefully. Their victims' necks were not broken when they dropped. This was dirty work, and they wanted to get it over with quickly. They usually paid to have their killing done, but even a hardened outlaw would not stoop to hanging a woman.

Ella Watson stood in the way of ambitious cattle ranchers. She had a choice piece of property on Horse Creek with water rights, bottomland for hay, and a good winter range. With her husband Jim's contiguous property, the couple controlled a mile of the creek. Her land had been open range that rancher Albert John Bothwell and his fellow ranchers considered theirs. At first, Bothwell was shocked that someone would be so bold, especially a woman. Everyone knew what he thought of nesters. He tried to buy her land but she wasn't interested in selling. Next Bothwell tried intimidation and threats, even breaking down her fences and running off her cattle, but this woman was made of sturdier stuff and could not be scared off.

Watson became a victim of greed and arrogance. Powerful men in the Wyoming Stock Growers Association who had money and connections were able to thwart justice. The guilty would not pay for their crimes. In fact, for many years they would be lauded as heroes. A hardworking farm girl from Kansas who had dared to live her dream would be sacrificed and reconfigured into the bitch, Cattle Kate. It took some doing because this was not the kind of branding cattlemen were used to, so they hired experts.

ELLEN LIDDY WATSON

Born Ellen, she went by Ella. Those who knew her said she was an affable woman with blue eyes and brown hair. There are many stories about her, but not all of them agree. Historians wish they knew more, because there are question marks, if not some blurred lines between facts and story. When a person has been badly treated by history, sometimes there is a rebounding effect. That person is recounted in a more positive light to make up for the unfairness. Nevertheless, Ella was a good woman, but she

Ella Watson, better known as Cattle Kate. PUBLIC DOMAIN/WIKIMEDIA COMMONS.

was not a saint. Most folks considered her good looking; she stood about 5 feet 7 inches tall and weighed about 160 pounds.

She was born in Canada, probably around July 2, 1860. Her family moved to Kansas in 1877. Like many farm children, she learned to read and write at country schools. The eldest of ten children, she helped around the house and tended her younger brothers and sisters. Considered a good catch, she married William Pickell, a farmer, on November 24, 1879. What looked like a promising future turned sour. When her new husband started drinking, he became abusive. Several times he beat her so badly she was embarrassed to leave her house because of the bruises. Each time Pickell sobered up, he told her how sorry he was and that it would never happen again. He would go for a while without drinking but the bottle seemed to win. The last time he beat her, he used a horse whip. She fled to her parents' farm and refused to go back. When he came to get her, she flatly told him it was over. They were later divorced.

She moved to Denver and stayed with her brother while she earned enough to move to Cheyenne, Wyoming Territory, in 1885. She did not like the city, and early in 1886 she relocated to Rawlings. Ella's dream was to have a place of her own, but first she needed to get a job. She went to work at the upscale Rawlings House, a boardinghouse/restaurant. This is where she met Jim Averell, who was traveling on business. He was impressed with his food and discovered that Ella, who was his waitress, had done most of the cooking. The two got acquainted. Later Jim offered her a business deal. He wanted someone to run his roadhouse. Ella's great cooking would bring in lots of business. The roadhouse was at a good location between Rawlings and Casper, besides the cowboys would ride for miles to get a fine home-cooked meal. Ella would have her own place to stay, and she would not have to worry about rent. While this is Ella Watson's story, it's important to mention that it's Jim Averell's story, too. He wasn't the two-bit pimp and hustler that the newspaper reports said he was. Averell was reconfigured and sacrificed along with Watson. Instead, he was a successful man in the Sweetwater Valley who was respected and liked. The roadhouse was a store, saloon, and restaurant. Canned goods, ammunition, flour, and other needed items were for sale, but Averell also had other business ventures so he was often gone and needed someone he could trust. It's important to mention Averell was the postmaster, a notary public, a Carbon County Justice of the peace, and an election judge. This hardly stacks up with the yellow press mythology and accusations promoted by the disfiguring fiction passed off as news. Averell understood Watson had been an abused woman who fled her home with little more than the clothes she wore. She needed to have something she could call her own. He helped her fill out and file the homestead application papers, and he likely advised her on her selection of land.

Then they fell in love. The thirty-nine-year-old widower Averell and twenty-nine-year-old divorcee Watson were secretly married. Only their close friends knew. If they were single, they could each file separately on two, 160-acre homesteads. After the allotted time each would own their land outright and then they could announce their union. The applicant had to be twenty-one or head of the house. A couple or a single head of the house was allowed 160 acres. A squatter-homesteader filed an application for 160 acres on surveyed government land. Then the applicant had to "prove up," meaning improve the land. After five years, the applicant could file for a deed. Yes, Averell and Watson were cheating, which was why they kept their true marital status quiet. This way the couple would get twice as much land. Averell understood that part of Watson's time would be working on her place. The government required improvements, so she built a small cabin and outbuildings and dug an irrigation ditch. Later she started a small herd. Eager to make as much money as she could, she made pies and mended for cowboys.

BUILDING HER RANCH IN WYOMING

When her neighbor John Crowder asked for help, she came immediately, because Mrs. Crowder was quite ill. Watson nursed the dying woman and did what she could to make her comfortable, made food for the family, cleaned the house, and tried to comfort the children. After his wife's death, Crowder was distraught and had no desire to stay in the Sweetwater Valley. Sending his younger children to stay with their aunt, Crowder left his eleven-year-old son, Gene, to be raised by Watson, while he went west to seek his fortune in the goldfields. He was never heard from again. Occasionally a cowboy would trade a calf for food, some pies, or to have his clothes mended. Likely, Watson didn't inquire too carefully about how the cowboy got the animal. In 1888, on a road between Casper and Rawlings, some men pushing a herd sold her some of their worn-down cattle. Apparently, they didn't think these cows could make the long journey to the goldfields. Watson got them for a good price and would fatten them up on her bottomland. John Bothwell didn't live far from her homestead and knew she had acquired a small herd and the circumstance of the sale. She'd had them all winter. Before he hung her, however, Bothwell would accuse Ella of stealing them from him. Both Watson and Averell had individually applied to get brands, but the Wyoming Stock Growers Association would not consider their requests. It was the association's way of controlling homesteaders. But Watson got lucky. When a small rancher decided to pull up stakes and move on, he sold her his brand for a good price. He had no love for the association, and he liked Watson and wished her well. She registered the LU brand in her name with the Carbon County Brand Commissioner sometime during March 1889. They would not let her register a new brand, but they could not keep her from purchasing an existing one. Having a brand legitimized her entry into ranching. Bothwell was furious when he heard the news. She kept her livestock bills of sale, her homestead application, and her brand registration in a safety deposit box in Rawlings.

All her earned extra money was spent building her ranch. At the same time, her foster family grew. Averell's teenage nephew, Ralph Cote, came from Wisconsin to stay at the roadhouse. Averell and Watson also collected another stray, John DeCory, who worked at the homestead and the roadhouse. Their good friend and neighbor, Frank Buchanan, worked for wages at the ranch. Perhaps just as important, Buchanan was a seasoned cattleman and was able to advise the couple on ranching and cattle purchases. Other than the men who hung her, he would be the last one to see either Watson or Averell alive. He watched them hang her. After Bothwell, and his ranching cronies, John Durbin, Ernest McLean, Robert Calbraith, Robert Conner, and Tom Sun had taken the couple away in a buckboard, Buchanan rode up to the roadhouse. The boys were upset, explaining that Averell and Watson had been taken at gunpoint. There had been hard words, and the ranchers also threatened the boys. Buchanan raced off and found them in a small draw up Horse Creek about to start the hanging; he fired shots with his pistol, but he only had a few bullets. They fired back with rifles and then he witnessed the murder. They followed him, but he outdistanced them and rode to Rawlings for County Sheriff Frank Hadsell. He was exhausted about twenty-five miles from town, so a friend took the message. Sheriff Hadsell collected a posse and a coroner and investigated the murder scene. After two-and-a-half days in the hot July sun, the bodies were bloated, blackened, and covered with flies. The smell was nauseating. The couple was cut down and taken back to the roadhouse and buried in a common grave. The sheriff and the coroner collected testimonies from the boys and Buchanan; the sheriff was committed to see justice done. He arrested all six men who freely admitted they had hung the two rustlers. Ironically, the six ranchers were charged with manslaughter and were able to bail each other out. This seemed a breach of justice because they had admitted to hanging the couple, but there was no bail for murder and it wouldn't seem right to have six respectable ranchers in jail.

REBRANDING ELLA WATSON AS CATTLE KATE

When the Wyoming Stock Growers Association learned the lynchings had happened, they went into a defense posture. They were pleased that Watson was dead, but it would have been better if it had been done more carefully. Nevertheless, the lynching had sent a strong message to the homesteaders that the association meant business. Any kind of rustling was a serious offense and required the stiffest, immediate punishment—whether it was legal or not. At all costs, the six men should not be convicted and should have the best defense their money could buy. Next, they would buy off, scare off, or kill anyone who would be detrimental to their case. They needed the help of George Henderson. He was not only their best stock detective, but he was also a fixer who had served them well in the past. He received the message, "Take care of it." Henderson would start by orchestrating damage control. He would begin by arming the cattlemen with the best news coverage money could buy. There were two important newspapers in Wyoming Territory, the *Cheyenne Sun* and the *Cheyenne Daily*. He would visit both editors because their papers had the largest circulations and were major news links with the East Coast. Each were fiercely competitive papers and took pride in outscooping the other. Henderson understood the Wyoming Stock Growers Association needed to control the story and show the action was justified—after the fact. These two important territorial voices would create a trial by newspaper.

First he visited Ed Towse, the editor of the *Cheyenne Sun*. Henderson knew both men, and knew Towse was not only pro-cattle but was also a personal friend and a drinking buddy with most of the large ranchers. Of course he would help. Henderson explained the situation. Towse sensed this story would go national His paper headlined, "A DOUBLE LYNCHING" with subheadlines "Postmaster Averill and Wife Hung for Cattle Stealing" and "They were tireless Maverickers who defied the law." Next Henderson visited E. A. "Archie" Slack, the editor of the *Cheyenne Daily*. Not to be outdone, Slack jumped in. Between the two creative writers, Watson was renamed Cattle Kate, and the legend was spun. It was quickly picked up by the *National Police Gazette*. Cattle Kate became quite a character. The same false stories were reprinted again and again. In a fight she "knocked him down with a stunning left-hander and lashed him with her riding whip till he begged for mercy." The *Salt Lake Herald* reprinted the story, saying "of masculine physique, she was a dare-devil in the saddle; quick on the shot; an adept with the lariat and branding iron."

To do this it's necessary to reconstruct her entire psychological profile, ignore the truth, and teach the lie. She can no longer be the kind, affable Ella Watson most folks knew. She must become the bitch—Cattle Kate—not only lower than the angels but a minion from the world of shadows. They started by making her less than a woman; the creation so vile that every Victorian assumption was challenged. Of course she was a whore, a cattle rustler, and a leader of outlaws. But she was worse; Cattle Kate was a procurer and a corruptor. In the end, hanging was all that could be done. She sold all that was good, if she ever knew what good was, because her role was deceptive. As sad as it was, the ranchers had no other choice. They executed out of a sense of honor. It was for the public good; they did it for the same reason they'd shoot a rabid dog near a school. They did it for the same reason they had to hang her pimp, Averell.

AFTERMATH

John Bothwell, John Durbin, Ernest McLean, Robert Calbraith, Robert Conner, and Tom Sun were never brought to justice. When the trial convened, no witnesses appeared in court. There is speculation, but it was assumed that Frank Buchanan, a key witness, was under protective custody but fled for his life. He may have been murdered in Colorado. Gene Crowder disappeared, or more likely, was murdered. Ralph Cole died just before trial, probably poisoned. John DeCory, who helped around the roadhouse and ranch, fled for his life. And Bothwell ended up with both Watson's and Averell's ranches.

12

TEDDY ROOSEVELT

"THAT DAMNED COWBOY" WAS A BULLY BUSTER PRESIDENT

I have always said I would have not been President had it not been for my experience in North Dakota.

Theodore Roosevelt

DAKOTA TERRITORY

Theodore Roosevelt had been in the saddle for several days exploring the Badlands of eastern Montana. Somewhat saddle weary, he hoped to spend the night in Mingusville, Montana Territory. His ranch in Medora, Dakota Territory, was at least thirty-five miles away and it was late. He booked a room at the Nolan, the only hotel in town; after checking in, he went to the hotel bar to get a meal.

"I heard one or two shots . . . as I came up." Pacing up and down in front of the bar, a "shabby" man wearing a big hat had "a cocked gun in each hand." He had killed the clock on the bar, "which had two or three holes in its face." Roosevelt wrote that the barkeep "was wearing the kind of smile worn by men who are making believe to like what they are doing." It was a cool evening, and hoping to be unobtrusive, Roosevelt slipped in and took a seat near the stove. The man with the cocked pistols was not about to leave him alone. He yelled, "Four Eyes!" Roosevelt hoped laughing it off would be enough, but it wasn't. In his notes, Roosevelt observed,

Theodore Roosevelt standing next to a horse, near Medora (North Dakota). Taken by T. W. Ingersoll. HARVARD UNIVERSITY LIBRARY, THEODORE ROOSEVELT COLLECTION 520.14-007

the man with the pistols was "a would-be bad man, a bully, who for one moment was having things his own way." The fellow came over to Roosevelt's table and yelled, "Four Eyes is going to treat." Roosevelt was dusty from the trail, an obvious stranger, and, worse, wore glasses, which was considered unmanly. Roosevelt tried to laugh it off, again, but the ploy failed. There was only one way to handle a bully: confront him head-on. As the man with the pistols leaned over, insisting on drinks, Roosevelt said, "Well, if I have to, I have to." He started to stand and looked past the drunk, feigning some measure of compliance. Then he responded with a quickness that surprised everyone in the room. Without the usual bantering foreplay, Roosevelt wrote, "I struck quick and hard with my right just to one side of the jaw, hitting with my left as I straightened out, and then again with my right." Roosevelt must have hit the bully with some force because both guns discharged as he crumpled. Fortunately, no one was hurt, and Roosevelt quickly disarmed the man. Several grateful patrons drug the unconscious fellow outside and secured him in a shed. Roosevelt finally got his supper as the men at the bar congratulated him. The troublemaker apparently took a freight train out of town early the next morning. Roosevelt did not like bullies.

In his pocket diary, months earlier, he had scribbled, "The light in my life has gone out!" But a heartbroken-hearted Roosevelt wasn't the sort of man who ran from fate's demons or wallowed in self-pity. He felt he had to face his grief by confronting it head-on. He had come West, rebuilding himself anew in the American wilderness. He wanted to be a cattleman in the twilight of the frontier while there was still open range and a handful of buffalo. He found the natural world, especially the wilderness, rejuvenating and as a city dweller, relished the physical challenge of living outdoors. Before he was twenty-five, he had lived an eventful life: He had been elected to the New York legislature and become a player in the national Republican Party. However, on Valentine's Day, 1884, he'd abruptly lost his wife and mother. After finishing his professional obligations, he left his Manhattan mansion for his ranch in Dakota Territory, a three-room cabin built from ponderosa pines. Now he would rebuild and reshape himself, doing this by becoming a cowboy.

THE ROOSEVELT MYTH

There was something rugged and uniquely American about the cowboy mystique and the West. There is certainly a sizeable gulf between a real cowboy and the "cowboy myth," but it was the myth that captured the American imagination. There was something about the lone cowhand, the rugged individual who followed his cowboy code of honor, the lone warrior who did hard things and stood up for right and for the common man, even against fierce odds, and who fought bullies and protected those in need protection. A cowboy was not born; he was made the way Roosevelt reimagined himself, the way America could reimagine itself.

What the young Roosevelt learned from his cowboy days in the Dakota Territory became the foundational roots of the Roosevelt mythology, which he wholeheartedly believed, and from which he spun his books and articles. He didn't promote himself as the rich kid of privilege but as the guy on the horse in a cowboy hat. We must consider several things when we focus on Theodore Roosevelt. He was a romantic driven by a profound belief that the Founding Fathers' republican values—and democracy—was the finest way to build the American Dream. He was a capitalist not a socialist, but he was a man of the people, a populist who felt that the Gilded Age and robber barons had made it arduous for the average person to share the dream of prosperity and democracy. He felt the large businesses and trusts had created unethical monopolies, and governmental action, not unchecked laissez-faire capitalism, was the answer.

To understand him, he must be looked at within his historical and cultural narrative as a real person. At times our relationship with Roosevelt is complicated. He was dynamic, charismatic, and sometimes contradictory. Historical and popular opinions have ebbed and flowed, and yet, Roosevelt nearly always appears among the top five presidents of the United States—usually as number four. He made big, big mistakes, but he made big wins, too. He could be self-promoting, bold, and reckless. He was often an ideologue and an imperialist. Roosevelt was not above shenanigans. One example is his sidestepping Colombia and promoting the new nation of Panama to get a canal built. But he was intrepid and relentless when as a trustbuster he took on the Wall Street moguls.

BORN TO MONEY AND HOME ON THE RANGE

Theodore Roosevelt Jr. was born October 27, 1858, in New York City. His wealthy family traced their ancestry to the first Dutch who settled Manhattan. The Roosevelts were considered old money—sometimes called the "Knickerbockers" named after the Dutch settlers who wore knickers. Roosevelt was a thin, pasty little boy afflicted with a severe case of asthma and stomach disorders. At night he slept propped up by pillows or in a chair so he could breathe. Because his health was precarious, he was educated by tutors. Always a voracious reader, he developed an intense fascination with the natural world. His notebooks were filled with comprehensive notes and drawings of what he'd been studying, from fireflies to flowers to ants. He observed, researched, and wrote articles and essays on what he had learned. Reading about the American West—his heroes

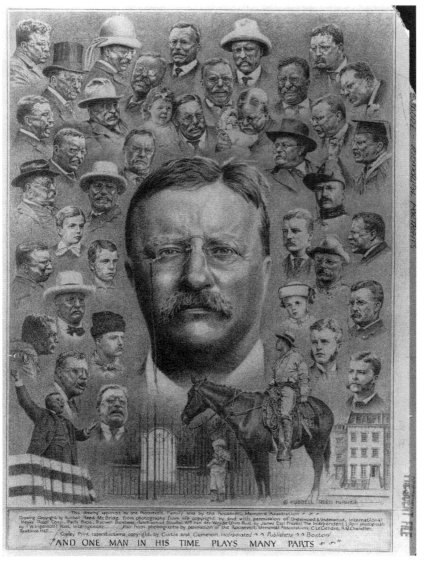

Print showing montage of drawings of Theodore Roosevelt from childhood to old age. LIBRARY OF CONGRESS PRINTS AND PHOTOGRAPHS DIVISION WASHINGTON, DC 20540 USA HTTP://HDL.LOC.GOV/LOC.PNP/PP.PRINT

were Daniel Boone and David Crockett—he dreamed about adventures, but the majority of the time he stayed in his room, so he wouldn't break into uncontrolled fits of coughing. Once when shooting a small-caliber boys' rifle, he noticed others hitting targets he couldn't see. Mentioning this to his father, his eyes were examined. They discovered he was near-sighted and needed glasses.

As a twelve-year old, Roosevelt was thin, wimpy, and bespectacled. He had a high, squeaky voice and was a know-it-all. He was teased and sometimes beat up by the boys in the neighborhood. As someone who loved adventurous swashbuckling novels, he felt intimidated and shamed. His father, Theodore Roosevelt Sr., told him he'd have to stand up to bullies and learn how to fight them head-on. However, first, his father advised him, he needed to do battle with another bully that plagued him, his health. The best way to do this, Theodore Sr. recommended, was to become physically fit. From his father, he developed a lifelong love of exercise and the virtues of a "strenuous life." "Theodore," his father told him, "You have the mind, but you have not the body, and without the help of the body the mind cannot go as far as it should. I am giving you the tools, but it is up to you to make your body." His father hired what today would be called personal trainers. Theodore Jr. began with boxing lessons to learn how to defend himself; he lifted weights, ran, and hiked; and working consistently and fully, he became physically fit.

MARRIED AND POLITICS
In 1880, the newly minted Harvard graduate married the lovely Alice Hathaway Lee, the daughter of a wealthy socialite from Boston. After a world tour, the ambitious Theodore Roosevelt was elected to the New York legislature at age twenty-three. He had a promising career in public service, being one of the youngest men elected to the New York legislature. He ran on an anticorruption platform, taking on the robber baron, Jay Gould, and New York City corruption. Being young, wealthy, and only two years out of college, he was a bit cheeky. He dressed like a hip boulevardier and not a conservative like his colleagues. His biting diatribes against corruption hit too close. Some of his political enemies and their allies in the press, hoping to discredit his platform, started calling him a

by names like "Jane Dandy" and "the Exquisite Mr. Roosevelt," and there were other more vulgar, sexual slanders. He was also called "Oscar Wilde," referring to Wilde's unveiled homosexual antics during his American tour in 1882. When one of the most outspoken politicians threatened him with violence, Roosevelt approached him, saying, "By God! If you try anything like that, I'll kick you, I'll bite you, I'll kick you in the balls, I'll do anything to you—you'd better leave me alone." As he wrote later, "We despise and abhor the bully, the brawler, the oppressor, whether in private or public life."

VALENTINE'S DAY TRAGEDY

It should have been a blissful time. Alice had given birth a few days earlier than expected, so Roosevelt rushed home. It was Valentine's Day, 1884. He found he had a healthy baby girl, but Alice was semicomatose. He held her until she died hours later from a kidney problem that was undiagnosed during her pregnancy. On the same day, Roosevelt's mother, Martha Stewart Bulloch Roosevelt, "Mittie," died from what might have been typhoid fever. Hoping to assuage or bury his grief, Roosevelt, now widowed with an infant, dove into his governmental duties, specifically the corruption in New York City government. He was also an up-and-coming player in the national Republican Party. But he backed the wrong man. Dealing with political disappointment and sorrow, he became disillusioned after the national convention. Leaving his daughter with his sister, Roosevelt boarded a train for a ranch he'd purchased in the Dakotas. He hoped against hope living a rugged outdoor life would help him heal. Some thought this a sudden and startling move, but in letters as early as April, he wrote about his need to rebuild himself, living a ranching life, hunting big game, and breathing fresh air.

LOOKING LIKE AN EASTERN "DUDE"

He outfitted himself as a typical eastern "dude," playing at becoming a cowboy. A simple review of his cowboy or hunter studio images is entertaining. The buckskin outfit photo, taken in 1883 (or maybe 1884) has him decked in leather with obligatory fringes. Such clothing would cost a fortune by frontier standards—at least three months wages for a cowhand, but Roosevelt was hoping to capture the look of his frontier heroes, David Crockett and Daniel Boone. Keep in mind, Roosevelt's belt knife in the image was custom made at Tiffany's in New York City, and he removed his glasses, so he looked more manly. When he stepped off the train in Medora to escape city life in 1884, he was the image of a clueless imposter attempting to look like a cowboy. He told his sister in a letter, "I now look like a regular cowboy dandy, with all my equipment finished in the most expensive style." At the time emaciated Roosevelt was five-feet, eight-inches, 135 pounds. He looked so skinny, one cowboy said you could "span his waist with your thumbs and fingers."

HIS FIRST ROUNDUP

Roosevelt didn't want to cheat himself out of any piece of the cowboy experience, including the spring roundup. It was a cowboy rite of passage. In 1885, he joined with other ranchers and cattlemen in the Little Missouri Valley as they explored the coulees, canyons, and draws for a hundred miles, searching for strays. Roosevelt didn't attain the authentic image of cattlemen on the roundup, so a couple of Texas cowhands nicknamed him "Storm Window." The Harvard Phi Beta Kappa ignored it out of initial politeness at first, but when the jeers began to border on bullying, he walked over to an offending Texan and called him out. Roosevelt told him they were going to fight right now! The man sensed this overdressed easterner wasn't posturing. Roosevelt said something like "put up or shut up and be prepared to back it up with your fists." Then, in a typical Roosevelt manner, he offered the cowhand an honorable way out. He said something like it's going to be a long roundup, so "we can be friends, or we can fight, your call." They became friends.

THEODORE AS LAWMAN

Roosevelt was fond of saying, "To submit tamely and meekly to theft or to any other injury is to invite almost certain reposition of the offense." On March 24, 1886, Theodore hunted down thieves who took his rowboat and brought them to justice. It was the stuff of legends—as if he was living out his childhood dreams. Roosevelt was a deputy for "Hell Roaring" Bill Jones in Dakota Territory, in 1885–1886, but that would not have

Theodore Roosevelt with silver-mounted bowie knife from Tiffany's, 1885.
PUBLIC DOMAIN/WIKIMEDIA COMMONS.

mattered. He believed that vigilante justice was his constitutional right. At any rate, it was a quintessential act for the man who would become the cowboy president. Like a western code hero in a final act, he was the cowboy turned lawman. His life narrative shows that he not only tamed his section of the West, but he was also able to tame himself.

The loss of the boat, valued at $25, was inconvenient, but was it that big a deal? Most ranchers couldn't afford to take a couple of weeks during spring to chase a petty thief; serious cattlemen were attending to their cattle. His action was similar to picking up a nickel instead of the dollar beside it. Nevertheless, he and his men quickly built another boat. They trusted the craft enough to go one hundred miles downstream through a treacherous spring thaw. Roosevelt described the dangerous conditions. "It [a huge chunk of ice] moved slowly, its front forming a high crumbling wall, and creaming over the like an immense breaker on the seashore. We could hear the dull roaring and crunching as it ploughed down the riverbed."

So Roosevelt could have a great adventure, he disregarded the dangerous, if not reckless, situation he placed himself and his cowboys in. If he or one of his cowhands fell into the icy water with heavy winter clothing, boots, holstered handguns, and filled ammo loops, it would have been fatal. He was playing a cowboy lawman as he would later play at war while leading the Rough Riders in Cuba. Some days, he commented, the river was frozen until midmorning. He said, "There was very little amusement in combining the functions of a sheriff with those of an arctic explorer." But he was having the time of his life. Finally, Roosevelt's party found the thieves and captured them at gunpoint. After a prolonged ordeal, he successfully brought the thieves to justice. Like a hero in a Shakespearean play during the final act, Roosevelt's disordered universe was once more brought back into alignment. Never mind that he and his men risked their lives for a $25 rowboat. Additionally, Roosevelt paid a man with a wagon to transport that small boat one hundred miles upstream to his cabin. He had paid his hired men much more than the cost of the boat; they surely weren't getting ranch work done. But from a PR perspective, which he could hardly consider at the time, the press and notoriety would become invaluable in branding his legend.

THE CHALLENGE

When Roosevelt returned to his ranch after a visit to the East, he found he'd been challenged to a duel:

My dear Roosevelt:
My principle is to take the bull by the horns. Joe Ferris [one of Roosevelt's men] *is very active against me and has been instrumental in getting me indicted by furnishing money to witnesses and hunting them up. The papers also publish very stupid accounts of our quarreling—I sent you the paper to N.Y. Is this done by your orders? I thought you were my friend. If you are my enemy, I want to know it. I am always on hand as you know, and between gentlemen it is easy to settle matters of that sort directly.*
Yours very truly,
Morès
I hear the people want to organize the county.
I am opposed to it for one year more at least.

The man who challenged Roosevelt, the Marquis de Morès, was his neighbor whom he had met on social occasions. The marquis was a hot-tempered Frenchman, a cattle baron, who had been in several duels. At the time of his challenge, he was facing legal troubles for a previous killing. He was a graduate of a French cavalry academy. In 1882 he had married a wealthy American woman. He owned a private railcar for their traveling, and he had a multimillion-dollar line of credit. His goal was to transform his ranch into a cattle kingdom, one including a butchering facility. He christened the local town Medora after his wife—obviously using a bottle of champagne.

Roosevelt told his friends he refused to meet the challenger with sword or pistol. If they met, it would be with Winchesters. However, he hoped to avoid a duel because the insult to the baron's honor was based on a false assumption. Nonetheless, if honor demanded a fight, he'd fight. His reticence was wise. This wasn't a barroom brawl with a drunk or getting the drop on a few petty rowboat thieves. This was a man who'd been formally trained and who had killed before. Roosevelt replied:

Most emphatically, I am not your enemy; if I were, you would know it, for I would be an open one and would not have asked you to my house nor gone to yours. As your final words, however, seem to imply a threat, it is due to myself to say that the statement is not made through any fear of possible consequences to me; I too, as you know, am always on hand and ever ready to hold myself accountable in any way for anything I have said or done.
Yours very truly,
Theodore Roosevelt

This was not a battle Roosevelt wanted to fight, and it was a battle he could avoid. He didn't back himself in a corner. If we scrutinize his language, we see the craftmanship in this message. Note the last line, "accountable for . . . anything I have done or said." Roosevelt was back East but he gave himself and the marquis an honorable way out.

In his books, he used this anecdote to demonstrate his prudence. The difference was easily worked out and the duel never took place. A cowboy can and will fight, Roosevelt demonstrated, but not if he doesn't have to. Both men had kept their honor. Later, in an unprecedent action as president, he brokered and settled a major dispute between miners and mine owners in the same fashion.

Roosevelt would say that it's respectable to defend yourself when necessary, but a fight was always to be avoided because consequences could be dire. Fighting was a recognition that some things are worth standing up for. A cowboy, or a cowboy president, followed a code. He argued that a principled life was the only life worth living and a person has an obligation to live each day with courage. One must take pride in their work and do it.

William Tilchin, a Roosevelt biographer, observed the "big stick" method of diplomacy crystallized during the cowboy days. In Roosevelt's words "Do not get into a fight if you can possibly avoid it. If you get in, see it through. Don't hit if it is honorably possible to avoid hitting, but never hit soft. Don't hit at all if you can help it; don't hit a man if you can possibly avoid it; but if you do hit him, put him to sleep." On the range, he transformed his idea of a masculine hero. The Rough Riders were the physical manifestation of Roosevelt's new ideal: a synthesis of hardened frontier riflemen, skilled horsemen, and Texas Rangers, plus elite athletes from eastern colleges, including championship quarterback and steeplechase riders. "In personal daring and in skill as to the horse," he wrote, "the knight and the cowboy are nothing but the same Saxon of different environments."

NOT A REAL COWBOY, BUT HE LEARNED THE COWBOY WAY

We mustn't kid ourselves, Roosevelt was never a *real* cowboy, not in the vocational sense of the word. He was a great horseman and arguably among the best of the US presidents, but riding a horse doesn't make someone a cowboy. He went on the spring 1885 roundup in the Little Missouri Valley and beamed with infectious enthusiasm. He loved the excitement but never had the necessary skills to be a real cowhand. He couldn't throw a lasso, "cut" a herd, or brand a calf. What he did do was shoot fresh game for the chuckwagon. While he drank in the experience, he was in the saddle from dawn until dusk; thus, earning the respect of the cowboys. He would be considered a *gentleman* cowboy. He heartily embraced the cowboy spirit and helped define "cowboy mythology" as we know it today, but he was wealthy enough to live his dream and do cowboy stuff. He embraced the lifestyle, the culture, and the men. By his own admission, he said, "It took the snob out of him." Because he owned his own ranch and cattle, he could do ranch work as he pleased and leave the daily chores to his men. Besides his expensive clothing, he had curious habits that might seem a bit peculiar to the average cowhand. He brushed his teeth, slept on an inflatable pillow, had a rubber-coated bathtub, a bulging book bag, and read two books a week.

His longest ranch visit was four months, and most were shorter. He traveled back to New York to do business and see his daughter, but he also spent time big game hunting, including grizzly bears, black bears, buffalo, bighorn, elk, deer, and pronghorn. Consider the battery of weapons he brought for a four-month stay: two Colt .45 revolvers, a .45-caliber Winchester repeating rifle, a .50-caliber double-barrel Webley Express rifle, a .40-caliber Sharps rifle, and a 10-gauge shotgun—and don't forget the 1,700 cartridges and shotgun shells. During his ranch years, from

1883 until 1886, he spent 350 days at his ranch. He was the man paying the bills, after all, so he could do what he wanted. Roosevelt was embracing hunting and cowboying, but his other objective was to work on his writing, which was prolific. In addition to magazine articles, he authored three books, *Hunting Trips of a Ranchman*, *Ranch Life and the Hunting-Trail*, and *The Wilderness Hunter*.

THE STRENUOUS LIFE

We can always be certain of one thing: Roosevelt had an opinion. To give credit where it was due, he was not whimsical, and his opinions were well thought out and frequently illustrated by personal experiences. His "strenuous life" philosophy was not only a personal mantra but also a metaphor for how we should live as a nation. He believed in physical exercise. He studied jujitsu, boxed, canoed, and hiked. When he found out that he would be president, he and his family were on a walking tour in the Adirondacks. Roosevelt may have been the only president who skinny-dipped in the Potomac River during the winter.

"We can't shirk that which is difficult or hard if we want to be great, he told his children." In his famous letter Granville Stanley Hall, on November 29, 1899, he wrote, "I wish to preach, not the doctrine of ignoble ease, but the doctrine of the strenuous life." He added that life is "toil and effort." Success doesn't come with ease. Roosevelt would say that life is always a fight both physically and mentally. To oppose the challenges that face us, we need to be physically fit. He feared that because so many were living in cities and working in offices or factories, the American male was going soft. He claimed his great fear was that his own children would marry into the Gilded Age of luxury. What the country needed was to get back to the "strenuous life."

The American male, he said, was getting complacent. "My experience has been that weak and effeminate men are quite as apt to have undesirable qualities as strong and vigorous men." Such weakness will force us to submit to infamy. He added, "I disbelieve in brutality and cruelty. . . . A nation that cannot fight is not worth its salt, no matter how cultivated and refined it may be." The fact that it can fight often "obviates the necessity of fighting."

FIGHTING BULLIES AS PRESIDENT

"Now we've got that damned cowboy as president!" Were the famous words of Republican Chairman, Mark Hanna, as he disgustedly watched as Theodore Roosevelt, age forty-two, took the oath of office as the twenty-sixth president of the United States. President William McKinley survived approximately one week after an assassination attempt. The last thing the Republican Party wanted was the progressive Roosevelt in office. During the McKinley campaign, Hanna was opposed to making Roosevelt McKinley's running mate. He said, "Don't any of you realize there's only one life between this madman and the president?" However, the other Republican power brokers felt the best way to get the popular reformer and governor of New York neutralized was to put him on the Republican ticket as vice president.

Well, now that he was in office that "damned cowboy" had just begun. Roosevelt was a man of privilege, a leader of the Progressive movement, a child of the Gilded Age, and considered a traitor to his class. Not only had he gone West and lived among the vulgar and rough common folk of the frontier, but he was also proud of it. To the horror of the Industrialists and Wall Street—who had backed the laissez-fair McKinley—Roosevelt went to work on his agenda. He proposed a "Square Deal" that was good for all. His plan:(1) conservation of the natural resources; (2) control of corporations; and (3) consumer protection. These are sometimes referred to as the "Three Cs." A square deal, he argued, was "a more substantial equality of opportunity that rewarded all." He proposed a graduated income tax at a time the richest men in the world paid none. He begrudged no one getting wealthy, and he encouraged it as part of the American dream, but all needed a fair chance to go as far as they could on their own initiative. The genius of our system, he preached, was equal opportunity. He felt all people now and hereafter had rights to life, liberty, and the pursuit of happiness.

Like a cowboy on the plains cutting and herding cattle to market, the cowboy president targeted the robber barons, specifically unfair monopolies or trusts that created unfair competition and failed foster the "common good." In his view, the republic had lost its way and needed correction. The concentration of wealth since the Civil War was unprecedented. It created a class system: poor versus big business. These monopolies created superrich—the barons of banking, steel, railroads, and petroleum. In Roosevelt's day, 1 percent of the population owned 51 percent of the nation's wealth. John D. Rockefeller, the richest man in the world, owned 2 percent of the nation's gross national product. Roosevelt immediately filed an antitrust suit against what he considered a bad trust, Northern Securities, a railroad trust controlled by J. P. Morgan. It was broken up in 1904. Some of the targets of his forty suits included Standard Oil, Tobacco, and Meat Packers. Roosevelt was influenced by Upton Sinclair, the novelist who wrote *The Jungle.* It was a book about the Chicago meatpacking industry. Roosevelt investigated and was disgusted, finding that packers used diseased, contaminated, and rotten meat. They had also created an unfair monopoly. Roosevelt took on the "Beef Trust." On June 30, 1906, he signed the Pure Drug Act and the Meat Inspection Act.

Conservation was an uphill battle. "If we of this generation destroy the resources from which our children would otherwise derive their livelihood, we reduce the capacity of our land to support a population, and so either degrade the standard of living or deprive the coming generations of their fight to life on this continent."

Today, the Roosevelt legacy is taken for granted. His progressive ideologies positively influenced the direction of our country. Roosevelt established 150 national forests, fifty-one federal bird reserves, four national game preserves, five national parks, and eighteen national monuments on more than 230 million acres of public land.

HOW ROOSEVELT LOOKED AT THE CONSTITUTION

Equally important was Roosevelt's interpretation of the Constitution regarding how the president and the federal government could and should act. He expanded the role and powers of the government markedly. Previously, thinking suggested that the federal government *could* do what was specifically stated in the Constitution. Roosevelt's more modern view of the Constitution, however, was that the Constitution spelled out what federal government could *not* do, and it could act any way it felt necessary, if the Constitution had not specifically prohibited it. For example, conservation measures such as preserving land, antitrust legislation breaking up monopolies, and the expanding role of the United States in world politics.

Roosevelt had become part of the West in one of the best personal and political makeovers in the history of American politics. He understood what he had to do, and he did it. He understood public opinion, marketing, and leveraging media, but it would be wrong to assume he completely comprehended his image. If it looks like he was having fun, he was. We can decide whether we like what he became, but finally he was always a romantic who had windmills against which to tilt. He was a homebound invalid who used grit and unflagging effort to transform himself emotionally and physically. Born to wealth, he championed the little guy who wasn't getting a fair deal. Roosevelt saw beyond consumptive practices and recognized our natural resources would not last if we didn't implement conservation, and he was not afraid to lead from the front.

13

ELIZABETH POTTS

MURDERESS DISMEMBERS HER VICTIM AND IS THE FIRST WOMAN HUNG IN NEVADA

Hanged by the neck till you are dead.
—Elizabeth Potts's death warrant

ELKO, NEVADA, 1890

For Elko, Nevada, it was a public relations nightmare. For Elizabeth Potts, it was worse. She'd have the problematic honor of being the only woman hung in the state's history. Her story would also become mingled in a larger public discussion exploring capital punishment and gender equity. It was bad business hanging a woman, but they were going to do it. It was the sort of controversy officials dreaded. Every legal step had been taken. The courts and jury proved beyond reasonable doubt that Potts was part of a horrific murder triangle in nearby Carlin, Nevada. She and her husband, Josiah, had shot Miles Fawcett in the forehead and then chopped his body into pieces with an axe so they could bury his remains in their basement.

Because women were almost never hung in the West, Judge John Bigelow felt it necessary to clarify to the public and press why his sentence was so extreme: "The mind naturally recoils with horror at the thought that anyone can become so lost to the common instincts of humanity. To her, we can look to everything that is kind and gentle. We can scarcely conceive her capable of committing the highest crime."

On the morning of June 20, 1890, Reverend C. J. Porter conducted a perfunctory prayer meeting for the condemned. Then the couple was offered a stiff drink to steady their nerves. At 10:30 a.m., Sheriff L. R. Barnard read the death warrant. Elizabeth said, "I am innocent, so help me God!" The lawmen escorted the emotionless pair to the platform. Josiah wore his Sunday suit. Elizabeth wore her best dress, which was white and adorned with black silk bows on her throat and wrists. She felt it was important to look her best and maintain her dignity. On the scaffold the couple kissed awkwardly. Josiah was slender and short, and Elizabeth was tall and stocky. They formally shook hands. Then the deputy strapped their wrists and legs together and removed their shoes. Black hoods were secured about their necks. There were no last words. Around 10:45 a.m., Sheriff Barnard cut the tie that held the trapdoor. The lawmen would have their bodies cut down and in coffins before lunch. It had been what was called a "dirty hanging." Elizabeth's height and weight had been miscalculated. She dropped too far. Her dress was a bloody mess, but at least her head was still attached so it wouldn't have to be sewn back on.

Some fifty journalists and law enforcement officials had been invited as witnesses. Flurries of editorials preceding the execution were followed by a landslide of opinion pieces that fanned a spirited national debate. The *San Francisco Daily Reporter* explained in its editorial, "It is a dreadful thing to hang a woman, but not so dreadful as for a woman to be a murderer." Closer to home, an editorial in the local paper, the Elko *Weekly Independent*, argued that this was going too far; it "would not reflect any credit on Elko." Few questioned the guilt of the condemned, nor was it troubling that Joshua Potts would be hung. He was a man, after all, and deserved his punishment because it was understood his sex made him more accountable. On the surface, this debate appears to have been about the propriety of hanging a woman. After all, women were supposed to be a little lower than the angels: They were the weaker, gentler sex, and must be treated with deference.

HANGING A WOMAN

Elizabeth Potts's story, twisted in myth and gore, is an interesting study in our historical canon—especially because her trial was based on circumstantial evidence. However, before we explore the specifics of her narrative, let's look at it in a larger context. For example, consider the judge's remarks in the introduction and the two representative newspaper samples in the previous paragraph as we think about gender assumptions of her day. Such statements examine, in a guarded fashion, critical questions about *women* and *women's roles* in the tightly woven social fabric. It appeared many of the handy stereotypes were no longer satisfactory.

Social lines were blurring as the United States raced toward a new century as an emerging superpower. Like an aspiring national debutant coming out on the world stage, a maturing United States was self-conscious about its homespun image. A more-sophisticated East put its best cultural foot forward hoping to social distance itself from the caricatured "wild and woolly" West, its bumpkin sister states on the frontier. At the least, the eastern states hoped to assume the airs of a cultivated nouveau riche and were not shy about embracing and reflecting the fashionable trends and thinking of the European blue-blooded urbane. In the 1820s, a hip philosophic movement rooted in England jumped the Atlantic. It became influential in defining gender roles for the next three generations. Perhaps it showed how suave the former colonies on the East Coast had become.

We now refer to this sexist philosophy as "the Cult of Domesticity" and "the Cult of True Womanhood." It was a pseudoscientific ideology that argued why men were morally, intellectually, and physically superior to women. It's nothing less than a trendy twist on Aristotle's discussion of public and private spheres. Men being more capable were suited for public spheres of government, reasoning, money, education politics, law, scholarship, and property ownership. Women, conversely, who were less capable, were suited for private spheres of home, motherhood, domestic chores, child-rearing, and pleasing their husbands. A "true woman displayed the virtues of filial piety and dignity; she understood her role was submissiveness to her husband," an order assigned by God. She must demonstrate all the homely virtues and not attempt a man's work for which she was

145

ill-suited. After all, the argument continued, a woman was not capable of "deep thinking," so novels and fiction ought to be avoided because such ideologies might confuse her thinking and blur her focus. Furthermore, readings should be religious- or moral-based. An example might be the immensely popular, dripping-sweet, 1854 narrative poem, *The Angel in the House: The Wife's Tragedy*. Here are a few lines:

> Man must be pleased; but him to please
> Is woman's pleasure; down the gulf
> Of his condoled necessities
> She casts her best, she flings herself.

Such cursory classifications might work nicely at Beacon Hill or at Manhattan tea parties but not on the frontier.

A WESTERN PERCEPTION OF WOMEN

It's natural that gender perception spun a slightly different orbit in the West, illustrating some of the subtle and not-so-subtle differences between Eastern and Western attitudes. Of course, we're looking at generalizations as we take a cultural snapshot. Certainly, women were still romanticized and real measures of equality were only looming on the horizon. However, a Western man's attitude was more pragmatic and slightly less chauvinistic. Women had value and were looked on as helpmeets, if not as partners. White women were first enfranchised in the West and were among the first to have voting rights, hold public office, and own property. There were male and female role orientations, but necessity demanded frequent crossing of gender lines. On overland trails, ranches, and farms, frontier women were expected to step beyond domestic roles of child-rearing, bible reading, cooking, and laundry. They drove wagons, rode horses, hitched teams, rounded up strays, plowed fields, defended cabins, and worked in the field. While men were away gathering cattle, hunting, earning cash money, or fighting Indians, women might be alone for months. They were familiar with shotguns and not afraid to use them. In 1854 in Washington Territory, for example, a legislator proposed a suffrage bill; it was defeated by one vote. On December 10, 1869, the governor of Wyoming Territory signed a bill granting women the right to vote. On February 12, 1870, Utah Territory followed suit. Ironically, before 1914, all states west of the Rockies had women's suffrage. East of the Rocky Mountains, except for Kansas, this was not the case. Western women had found a voice—heavily influencing the Mann Act in 1910, making prostitution illegal and paving the way for prohibition.

GOING WEST WAS A FRONTIER TRADITION

The West might be the land of promises when it was tamed; however, the payment was sweat, blood, and isolation. The first waves were generally populated by young, single men seeking their fortunes or quenching their restlessness before settling down. Examples are mountain men, fur trappers, soldiers, miners, loggers, rail builders, and cowboys. Married men were more likely to be in the later waves with their families heading to a promised land, perhaps on the Camino Real, the Mormon Trail, or the Oregon Trail. There was a viable frontier tradition making western movement not only possible but an accepted option. The great unknown offered economic advantages to the bold, the daring, and the risk-takers. Until the frontier was at least partly tamed, it was not suited for women. At the least, the new land was an opportunity for lower- and middle-class men to better their station. The land itself often became the reward. Others, of course, came West with specific dreams of forging a new home and planned to have their wives join them when it was safer for decent folk, a crop was planted, the Indians were run off, or a cabin was built.

The immensity of the land had been a great insulator, and men greatly outnumbered women—a scarce commodity. The current thinking held that even a bad woman could be useful—and was a hell of a lot better than no woman at all. Once a lonely mountain man walked thirty miles to see a young mother and offered her $50 if he could hold her baby. During the California Gold Rush, a miner paid $10 in gold for the first biscuit out of Luzena Wilson's oven.

Such a land demanded a steep learning curve with few safety nets. It was a bold adventure; a mistake could be fatal. There were no training classes or predictor exams to determine likelihood of success. It was a hazardous journey just to get there, wherever "there" might be. It took time and planning and outfitting to face a challenge so daunting and so expansive; some felt the solitude almost choked them. A survivor learned by doing, but the trick was staying alive long enough to understand how to live with, as well as, off the land. There were river crossings, hypothermia, thirst, hunger, starvation, grizzly bears, hostile attacks, accidents, disease, infections, outlaws, high prices, extreme weather patterns, and snakebites. Then add the inherent occupational dangers of mining, ranching, trapping, and cattle drives. Most started their new profession as "greenhorns" and either made do or died trying. There was plenty of hard work, but there were also loneliness and boredom—and thoughts of home. It was a wilderness that needed taming. In a boomtown or a camp, especially in the early days, there might be one hundred men for every woman. Women, *womanliness*, at least in theory, enjoyed an exaggerated glorification. There was sometimes distractions, gambling, cheap whiskey, and occasionally brothels, but rarely the cliched girl next door, your mother, or your sister.

THE CODE OF THE WEST IS AN HONOR CODE

Intentionally killing a woman, therefore, no matter what she'd done, was a damned waste. Beyond supply and demand, it was an ethical consideration. This ethos morphed into what is sometimes called the "code of the West." It was later hyperbolized by dime novels and films. It was, more correctly, an informal, unwritten, loosely constructed code of manners based on the honor system. Law and order took a while to catch up. Among the first tenets in this unwritten morality were those about how a woman should be treated. After all, if you were lucky enough to see a woman, you stood up out of respect and offered her your seat. You also tipped or took off your hat and helped her with packages or lifting something. Naturally, you'd speak politely, use good English, and not swear. You'd not smoke or spit because women are special. If a man was stupid or careless enough to insult a lady, you'd be honor bound to correct him. If he apologized, so much the better. If he didn't, you'd have to fight him to protect her honor. A man who violated a woman could be shot, strung up, or, if he was lucky, be the groom at a shotgun wedding. This implied morality, of course, only applied to "decent" white women—dancehall girls, whores, gambling women, salon hall girls, and hurdy-gurdy dancers were not included. Generally speaking, Black, Indigenous, or those of Asian or Mexican descent might be considered a lady on some occasions but only on an individual basis. Inside this code you had a God-given right to use deadly force in self-defense, defending your property, your family, or your home. You always helped someone in need and never let anyone leave your fire hungry; however, you could hang or shoot a claim jumper or horse thief. Last, but not least, if someone insulted you, your sacred honor demanded an apology or you were required to call him out. You always fought fair and never hit someone from behind . . . and you never shot someone in the back.

Frontier notions about how men perceived a woman seem thwarted. It helps if we peel off a few more layers of social strata and take a glimpse at the shadowy, comingled gender roots that are sometimes contradictory but insightful. It was a curious blend of medieval chivalry, Southern honor culture, Victorian values, and a biblical interpretation of original sin. A woman may not be an equal partner because she had been deceived in the Garden of Eden, but she was still a partner and an important helpmeet. But between the romantic notion of womanhood and the reality of life in a brave new land falls the pragmatic shadow of reality. In addition to her other duties, the helpmeet could take over the management of homestead, farm, ranch, or dry goods store.

In this conflicting ideology, it was not good for man to be alone because a woman was more than a tempering influence in a fallen world; she could make a heaven out of a hell. She could shoot her own rattlesnakes, keep the wolves from killing the milk cow, hoe the corn, and keep the cattle close if Indians were raiding nearby. Western men might believe she was the "weaker sex" and should be given a pass on, say, capital punishment, but they knew their female counterparts could be fiercely independent and tough, even if hanging seemed, well, distinctly unfeminine.

PROBLEMS IN ELKO, NEVADA

Two issues needed attention. Elko County ordered double gallows from Placerville, California. It would arrive by rail. The other issue, and one more difficult, was public safety because this was so controversial. Normally, a hanging was a peaceful, even social, event. It was usually scheduled

149

for Saturdays, making it easier for rural folks who were already in town getting supplies to attend. Families and friends would visit, maybe share a picnic lunch, and watch the main event. Businesses would close for an hour but reopen after the execution.

This was different. There weren't many peace officers in the county, the budget was tight, and crowds at a hanging could get out of control. When Charles Waller was hanged, eight thousand spectators escorted him to the gallows to bid him a swift journey to hell. Waller and his son had robbed and shot William Newland and then slit the throats of his wife and baby. When the coconspirators in the Abraham Lincoln assassination drew such a crowd, tickets to witness the execution were issued. Crowds choked the streets for miles and miles.

A few years earlier in Los Angeles County, California, there had been nearly as many vigilante as legal hangings. Dave Brown and Felipe Alvitre had been sentenced for two different murders. Each sought stays of execution while they appealed to the California Supreme Court. Such legal protocols and loopholes angered nearly two thousand justice-seeking, alcohol-fueled men. The general opinion was both men needed to be strung up right away. The mob rushed the jail, insisting the deputies hang the men immediately. The mob insisted that Alvitre, because he was a Mexican, be hung first. The noose broke and the stunned man fell to the ground. Annoyed with such an unprofessional performance by law enforcement, the crowd showed its displeasure by pelting the officers with stones. Someone got a new rope so the condemned man could be hung properly. The lawmen wisely slipped away, locking themselves in the courthouse.

After a few more drinks, however, the mob decided to hang Dave Brown. This time they wanted official leadership. All eyes fell on Mayor Steve Foster who'd been participating. Foster agreed but insisted he temporarily resign from his elected office. The former and future mayor, with some of his constituents, broke down the jail doors. This time they headed for the corral, which most agreed was a better venue. They remembered to bring a chair so Brown would get a proper drop. Because Brown was a white man, he was entitled to a last statement. Instead, the plucky Brown cheated a vigilante who had been given the honor of kicking the chair;

he jumped so he could die on his own terms. On another occasion, three hundred men in Los Angeles County showed up at the jail and demanded the deputies give up another convicted prisoner. The jail door had been reinforced, so it took nearly a half-hour for the vigilantes to break it down.

Elko law enforcement figured there was no way they could turn an angry crowd. In the name of public safety, they understood their duty. The Elizabeth Potts execution must be a "closed hanging," with only reporters present. The lawmen announced that executing a woman was so repugnant, so distasteful, it would offend the delicate and tender sensibilities of the women.

A GHOST IN THE BASEMENT

The couple's backstory, admittedly, gets a little confusing. What we must work with is a mixture of fact and folklore. There are firsthand and secondhand recollections, court records, and newspaper articles published before and after the trial. Potts, unfortunately, didn't leave letters or a journal, nor did she seem to have any close friends who could reconstruct a narrative. There are margins of error when we look at someone who lived 150 years ago. Elizabeth always proclaimed her innocence, but many of her champions showed up after her death. Variations in the telling of her story often reflect where the writer stood on capital punishment for a woman.

Let's begin with ghosts. I look on ghost stories with bemused skepticism but find them fascinating on some level. In confusing narratives or when we don't know all the facts, especially a grisly murder, adding a ghost narrative serves as a placeholder or a question mark. It gives a "workable why." It's a signal that seems to say, there's something we can't explain; there's some force "out there" that might be responsible. It's a device used throughout literature and historical speculation, such as in *The Iliad*, *Wuthering Heights*, and *Hamlet*. It seems fitting that there be an unrequited ghost. In Elizabeth Potts folklore, it's the restless ghost of Miles Fawcett.

The charming Mrs. Brewer, along with her husband and family, rented the home owned by the Pottses. Mrs. Brewer was also an aspiring writer. Her pen name was Busy Bee. In the tongue-in-cheek piece for the *Elk*

Free Press, June 21, 1890, she said, "it is a little exciting when one has the good luck to move into a veritable haunted house. Not many persons have such a thing happen to them these days. So far, the ghost hasn't scared any of us, but he is here just the same. Sometimes he taps on the headboard of the bed; other times he stalks across the kitchen floor, and then hammers away at the door, but no one is there." Apparently, the spirit couldn't rest until he was vindicated, and Josiah and Elizabeth were brought to justice. Mrs. Brewer, that Busy Bee, also suggested in her article, that the ghost "holds revels, upsets the pickles, and carries on generally." The ghost was so active that Mrs. Brewer had her husband, George, investigate. Using an iron rod, he probed the dirt in the cellar, where Mrs. Brewer assumed the ghost hung out. Under shelves in the corner, presumably shelves that held the pickles, he found the mortal remains of the ghost.

GUILTY AND REALLY GUILTY

According to a description in the Salt Lake paper, the *Deseret Weekly,* 1890, Elizabeth "had a large physique, with ruddy complexion, light blue eyes, and weighed 200 pounds." Josiah was said to be soft spoken, while his wife, euphemistically, was labeled strong-willed. They had five children and at one time lived in the Midwest. Both Elizabeth and Josiah were born in England. The couple married in 1863 and emigrated to the United States in 1865.

The couple had moved to Carlin, Nevada, where Josiah worked for the railroad. Accounts seem to imply the marriage may not have been made in heaven. The couple had known Fawcett for some time, probably in Wisconsin. According to the *Deseret Weekly,* Fawcett was a widower. In 1887 he purchased a ranch near Carlin, Nevada, that was called Hot Springs. He was also a carpenter. Elizabeth baked his bread and cleaned his clothes, and he "stayed" or rented a room at the Pottses' home in town. One story says that Fawcett had some information on Elizabeth, who, we are led to believe, was no angel. The *Deseret Weekly* called it "unpleasant details of her former career." The couple reportedly agreed to pay Fawcett a certain sum to keep him quiet because he was blackmailing them and demanding "services" rendered or money. Other accounts hint that Elizabeth sold more than bread. It was also suggested that maybe Josiah and

Elizabeth Potts. PUBLIC DOMAIN/WIKIMEDIA COMMONS.

Elizabeth were not legally married, and at one point, she may have been married to Fawcett. Another thread is that Elizabeth and Josiah had been separated. She went to California and wed Fawcett via a marriage broker; reportedly Elizabeth was paid $105. Then Fawcett found out she was still married to Josiah and threatened to reveal her bigamy. As a result, he was blackmailing them. Another thread suggests the couple borrowed money from Fawcett, and he was having a hard time collecting what he was owed.

There's something interesting about these accounts. Look at the ad hominem jabs. When we look carefully at the information—and admittedly we're drawing from a shallow pool of information—her scenario doesn't read like history; instead it reads like a series of crafted arguments meant to draw us to the conclusions that Elizabeth was not just guilty but that she was super guilty. Add the postscript: She was a rotten person, too. Unlike Cattle Kate who was lynched by large ranch vigilantes, Elizabeth Potts was investigated by professional lawmen, given due process in the courts, and legally hanged. This little tarring of her name helped make the disgusting duty of hanging a woman more palatable.

CONVINCING CIRCUMSTANTIAL EVIDENCE?

Fawcett decided to collect what the Potts owed him. He mentioned to friends that he was afraid to confront them by himself, so he took a friend, J. P. Linebarger. They stopped by the Pottses' home on the afternoon of January 1. Linebarger later suggested Fawcett had a $100 or more in cash, a hefty sum in those days, because Fawcett paid him a $5 debt from his bankroll. Linebarger further suggests, surprisingly, the couple was friendly so Fawcett dismissed him. He'd been invited to have a few drinks and stay the night. This was the last time anyone saw Miles Fawcett alive.

The next day, Fawcett's friend inquired about his whereabouts. Josiah Potts reportedly told Linebarger their friend had urgent business back East and caught the 6 p.m. night train the previous evening. Such news was a surprise to his good friend. Not satisfied, Linebarger asked the sheriff to investigate. After a couple more days, the sheriff drove out to the ranch and found Fawcett's cabin door wide open. It seemed a robbery had occurred. Some of the tools Linebarger had loaned Fawcett showed up at the Pottses' residence. It was curious, too, that Josiah Potts also had a bill of sale for not only Miles Fawcett's team and wagon but also for his ranch. The sheriff suspected something was out of place, but without more proof there wasn't much more he could do.

Fast-forward nine months to September. The Pottses moved to Rock Springs, Wyoming Territory, so they rented their Carlin home to the Brewer family. In December 1888, the Brewers needed more space, or was it, as some have suggested, the spooky spiritual prompting of an "other worldly" ghost? When Brewer was digging, he discovered pieces of a human body, and some pieces appeared to be burned. While the Brewers weren't forensic experts, they knewsomething was wrong. He called the sheriff who started putting the pieces, literally and metaphorically, together. Especially revealing was a burned trouser pocket with Miles Fawcett's pocketknife. This, along with other pieces of evidence, confirmed Sheriff Bernard's original suspicion. On January 24, 1889, he picked up Elizabeth and Josiah in Rock Springs. On the train ride back to Nevada, the sheriff said they, "gave the whole thing away." The evidence was incriminating. At times it seemed as if they made up a quick story and stuck with it.

During the interrogation, Elizabeth said previously, she'd caught Miles Fawcett in the barn having sex with her four-year old daughter. Fawcett allegedly threatened to kill both Elizbeth and her daughter if she told anyone. Satisfied that she'd keep silent, Fawcett continued to board at the Pottses' home while his cabin was being built. Elizabeth said she kept this dreadful secret from her husband because she was afraid. Later, though, her conscience was bothering her so she decided to write a letter to the sheriff.

On January 1, according to Linebarger, the Pottses warmly invited Fawcett in for drinks. According to their testimonies, their son, Charley Potts, entertained them with his guitar playing while they drank and chatted. At some point, as implausible as it might seem, Josiah Potts testified that in the middle of their celebration, he suddenly remembered he needed to get stamps out of Elizabeth's chest so he could fill out an order for a catalog he wanted to receive. Potts went into the bedroom and rummaged around in Elizabeth's chest for postage stamps. Instead he found the letter his wife was drafting. He wanted to go to the sheriff. Furious and ready for an impromptu confrontation, Josiah testified, "I took the letter in the other room. Fawcett was sitting near the window. I asked Fawcett what was meant by this!" He angrily handed the letter to Fawcett who read it and replied, "I must have been crazy." Then Josiah shouted something like, "I'll have him lynched!"

According to their narrative, the guilty, sobbing Fawcett confessed to the couple how sorry he was and pleaded for his life. He likely mentioned that he couldn't take back what he'd done, but he might be able to pay for their silence and go away. Perhaps he suggested killing himself. He may have told the couple use the money to help the poor girl get a new start and told them he'd sign over the deed to his ranch and team. He'd pay them all his cash and sign a bill of sale for his wagon and horses. Josiah apparently agreed they would keep quiet.

The drunken and remorseful Fawcett said he couldn't live with himself, and there was more arguing. He said he'd turn over his property. He asked for paper. He attempted to write the bills of sale but was so sad he couldn't do it, so he asked Elizabeth. He then signed them. Josiah threatened to have him hang, saying, "to hell with your note," and there was more arguing. At some point, Fawcett, familiar with the house, got the family revolver out of the cupboard and shot himself behind the ear—the bullet didn't exit the skull. Charley Potts was in the room and testified that Fawcett committed suicide.

Josiah sent his family to the other room so he could think. He wasn't sure what to do; it looked bad and he worried he'd be blamed. He fought a rising panic and moved Fawcett to their bed so he'd be out of the living room. Then he decided the cellar was a better choice. He buried Fawcett in a shallow grave. The next evening after dark, he said he went to the Fawcett's Hot Springs ranch where he searched for Fawcett's papers, which he found in a toolbox. He burned them. Later he dug up the body. He said he chopped Fawcett into smaller pieces with an axe and attempted to burn the body. He then reburied him. He stated his wife didn't help him in any way.

On January 28, they were bound over for the next grand jury. The sheriff's hypothesis was the couple got Fawcett drunk, and—possibly at gunpoint—talked him into signing over the deed to his ranch, as well as a bill of sale for his team of horses and wagon. Once the murderous couple had what they wanted, including his cash, one of the two conspirators neatly planted a bullet into Fawcett's forehead. Because it was New Year's Day, a gunshot in the kitchen would not seem out of place during the extended celebration. During the trial, Exhibits A and B, the bills of sale, were offered as evidence. There were questions regarding the validity of the signatures; the prosecution claimed they looked too much like

Elizabeth Potts's writing. Getting all of Fawcett's possessions was a serious motive for murder.

On February 13, they were indicted. They were tried on March 12, entering a plea of not guilty. By 8 p.m., the foreman, G. W. Philips said the jury found them "guilty of murder." Judge Bigelow sentenced them on March 22. The couple appealed to the supreme court and were granted a stay of execution, but in October 1889, this appeal was denied. A petition was submitted to the board of pardons requesting life imprisonment, but this also was denied. A second petition was again denied. Elizabeth then tried to commit suicide by slitting her wrists.

Perhaps the new gallows did too good a job. Josiah was small and got hung just fine. He twitched a little, but his neck was broken handily. He died fast and cleanly. It was a textbook-perfect execution. Elizabeth's hanging was marred by human error—maybe it was the hangman's first time with a rope. He was, after all, only a sheriff's deputy and not a professional executioner. He didn't take Elizabeth's large, heavy frame into consideration when he calculated the drop.

14

THE JOHNSON COUNTY WAR

WYOMING CATTLE BARONS HIRE TEXAS GUNMEN TO KILL HOMESTEADERS

State Senator Durban of Wyoming, who is here, says the [Wyoming] rustlers, who are in such numbers in his State that the ranchmen are unable to cope with them, are ruining the cattle business there, and a war of extermination is likely soon to begin against the thieves by stock-raisers. The rustlers not only steal steers and calves, but shoot cows. The rustlers are mostly desperadoes from Texas.
—*Sacramento Union*, December 8, 1891

JOHNSON COUNTY, WYOMING, 1892

They decided Nate Champion had to die. He had openly defied their authority and questioned the jurisdiction of the Wyoming Stock Growers Association. Even worse, he had united owners of small-sized ranchers and homesteaders—who were little more than rustlers—into scheduling an unsanctioned roundup. The cattlemen needed a man they could trust. His name was Frank Canton, a former sheriff of Johnson County who currently worked for the association as a cattle detective. He wasn't afraid of a little blood. Canton selected Joe Elliott, Tom Smith, and Fred Coats, proven men, to back him up. The four rode to a line shack on the fork of the Powder River to kill Champion and his hired hand, Ross Gilbertson.

Before dawn on Sunday, November 1, 1891, the four assassins tied their horses, took off their coats, and quietly slipped up to the door of the shack. They hoped to get a drop on the two men so they could lynch them. There was nothing better than a retaliatory hanging to show who was the boss, but two bullets would also work. Guns drawn, they busted through the door. The killers supposedly yelled something like, "Give up! We got you now!"

Apparently, their dramatic entrance took a fraction of a second longer than they'd planned, or maybe the two cowboys heard them. Champion is reported to have said, "What's the matter, boys?" He grabbed the Colt revolver under his pillow and was shooting before he'd finished talking. Gilbertson rolled off the bunk as a slug ripped a hole in his mattress. There were muzzle flashes, deafening echoes, and clouds of black-powder smoke. A bullet barely missed Champion's face—leaving a powder burn on his cheek. One of the killers took Champion's bullet in the side, a wound that would be fatal. Another gunman was nicked. The killers left in such a hurry they forgot to take their coat. One, presumably the wounded man, left his rifle. Champion recognized one of the shooters as Joe Elliott.

Gilbertson wisely decided to leave Johnson County. Elliott was charged with attempted murder. Two ranchers, John A. Tisdale and Orley "Ranger" Jones, friends of Champion, learned important information germane to the case and would be witnesses for the prosecution. To silence their testimony, both men were shot on December 1, 1891. Frank Canton was suspected of the murders. On February 8, 1892, Champion's critical testimony during the preliminary hearing was enough, and Elliott was bound over for trial in district court.

It began as an argument over open range. Or more precisely, an argument over how open range should be used and who had the right to use it. Several of the specific issues were water rights, grazing rights, cattle ownership, and homesteading. For nearly ten years, stockmen were free to do as they pleased on 97,914 square miles of Wyoming Territory. In 1870, the territorial population was nine thousand—a decade later the population had barely doubled. If there were land issues, the stockmen found intimidation and legal chicanery effective deterrents. However, as the population increased and more and more homesteaders filed legal claims on public land that was used as open range by stockmen, conflicts intensified. According to the stockmen, anything that conflicted with their interests was "rustling." By 1890 when Wyoming became a state, the population had tripled to 62,555. Cattleman graduated to bullets and ropes as the cold war with homesteaders (small ranching and farming concerns) heated up and hostilities intensified. Under the cloak of the Wyoming Stock Growers Association, owners of large ranches took punitive action. One example was hiring strong-armed stock detectives who created their own brand of frontier terror. Homesteaders fought back, and killings occurred on both sides. By 1891, owners of small ranches were organizing and proving to be an immediate threat as their numbers grew. Cattlemen saw their legal advantages slipping as homesteaders served on local juries. Even worse, legal decisions were not easily purchased. Range problems festering since the late 1880s had come to a bloody boil in the Johnson County War.

THE OPEN RANGE WAS A GARDEN OF EDEN

To put this in context, it's important to look back twenty-five years. Southeast Wyoming Territory would become a cattlemen's Garden of Eden. What was good for ranching, however, was a death knell for buffalo herds and American Indians. In 1867, Wyoming became a territory with the arrival of the railroad. A new rail town, Cheyenne, was born. It supplied the army and the gold rushes; however, its real wealth was in cattle. In 1867, the buffalo herds were estimated to be between 12 to 15 million. American consumers clamored for beef. At the same time, there were more than 5 million longhorns in Texas, many running wild and unbranded after the Civil War. Vast tracts of lush grassland were opening up as more of the tribes on the Northern Plains were "contained" on reservations. The concept, naturally, was simpler than it looked. In theory, all you had to do was round up a herd of Texas cattle, drive it north, and get rich. Promoting the territory, Nathan Baker, editor of the *Cheyenne Leader*, wrote on May 1, 1867, that Wyoming grass was "exceedingly nutritious" and water was abundant.

The Great Plains had once been called the Great American Desert—a vast, dangerous wasteland that pioneers *endured* on their way to the "promised land." Once the buffalo and the Indigenous groups were gone, this "wasteland" became the new "promised land." On May 10, 1868, General William Tecumseh Sherman wrote to General Philip Sheridan about the Sioux Indians following the buffalo herds, "I think it would be wise to invite all the sportsmen of England and America . . . this fall for a Grand Buffalo hunt and make one grand sweep of them all." The great herds had begun splitting because of the railroad, and the army knew the tribes would follow the buffalo. The army's noose around the "hostiles" would thus tighten; starvation would foster capitulation. Later that fall Sheridan wrote to Sherman that we must "make them poor by the destruction of their stock, and then settle them on the lands allotted to them."

By the 1870s, the buffalo herds were drastically reduced. General Sheridan would proclaim, "These men [buffalo hunters] have done more in the last two years and will do more to settle the vexed Indian question than the entire army." He suggested, "Then your prairies can be covered with speckled cattle." In less than ten years, most of the southern herd was gone; and the northern herds were rapidly following suit. On one Dakota "hunt," ten thousand buffalo were killed in a matter of days.

Cattle ranching on the Northern Plains was considered the new gold rush. In the early 1880s the book, *The Beef Bonanza and How to Get Rich on the Plains*, was a bestseller. In an 1879 issue of *Harper's Magazine*, an article suggested that a rancher with four thousand head of cattle should be able to clear more than $100,000 by the third year. That would be several million dollars today.

Investors from the East and Europe, as well as adventurous stockmen, hoped to carve out lucrative cattle empires in what had been buffalo country. Wyoming territory had been divided into five large counties, each about one-fifth of the present-day Wyoming. The bold with an entrepreneurial spirit, powered by investment capital, rushed to stake a claim. It wasn't easy, and ranches took on the aggressive characteristics of a medieval fiefdom *by necessity*, facing threats from tribal retaliation, rustlers, and nature. Ranch owners or their managers had to be powerful leaders and were often compared to feudal lords (nicknamed cattle barons, cattle lords, or range lords). There were no sheriffs or marshals or courts of law. The first ranches were cattle islands in a seemingly endless sea of grass. They backed up their "right with might." The famous Charles Goodnight, of the Goodnight-Loving Trail, took a herd to Cheyenne in 1868. He commented, "It was a period of chaos in the West . . . Indian raids, rustlers, crooks and land jumpers . . . there was very little law except what a man could enforce himself."

Because beef prices soared until 1885, the economic and political influence wielded by cattle barons was felt not only in prairie towns but also in large municipalities, reaching all levels of government. More than cattle were branded in Wyoming Territory. Large cattle concerns had their stamp on railroads, industry, newspapers, businesses, and law enforcement. Having more millionaires per capita, Cheyenne, Wyoming, was probably the richest city on Earth—one millionaire for every 375 people. In 1880, the ostentatious Cheyenne Social Club was built to cater to the wealthy. The wealthy might dine on oysters or Maine lobsters, sipping expensive French wines. A city lot in 1882 might sell for the outrageous price of $2,500, more than a range hand would earn in six or seven years.

ORGANIZING THE WYOMING STOCK GROWERS ASSOCIATION

The roots of the Wyoming Stock Growers Association grew into a powerful political force. The territory was created in 1869, and by 1870, a collective group of cattlemen were lobbying for their interests. In 1872 they formed the Laramie County Stock Growers Association, which would become the Wyoming Stock Growers Association. As Turrentine Jackson observed in *The Mississippi Valley Historical Review*, for all practical purposes the association was "the de facto territorial government" in Wyoming.

GREAT DIE UP OF 1886–1887

It was called the Great Die Up. For twenty years ranching was a lucrative business, but everything went terribly wrong, boom to bust. Many ranchers lost everything. Cattlemen who had dined at the opulent Cheyenne

Social Club, were riding the "grub line" hoping for supper or a place to stay. In spring 1887, dead cattle were stacked up like cordwood on the range. Investment capital disappeared.

For years, the winters had been mild and forgiving, while the summers had been cool and wet. Driven by larger profit margins, stockmen continued to increase cattle numbers on their range. In 1866 less than two inches of rain fell. Overgrazed grassland was barren and the cattle gaunt. Cattle had not put on any weight. The spring "green up" never came. The commander at Fort McKinney wrote, "The country is full of Texas cattle and there is not a blade of grass within 15 miles of the Post." Traditional water sources became trickles or dried up entirely. Next came sweeping prairie fires, consuming what little grass was left.

It was obvious the herds were in no shape for winter. Hoping to cut their losses, some ranchers put their "thin" cattle on the market. The glut caused Chicago prices to fall by half. Bad years were to be expected, so ranchers hoped to ride out the winter. Early snow and freezing weather came sooner than expected. Storms were relentless; temperatures reportedly dropped to 50 degrees below zero. There was so much snow, many spring roundups were impossible. There had never been a need to cut hay because herds wintered cold months by browsing. Losses were as high as 70 percent. During spring and summer 1887, the stench of decaying carcasses was unbearable. Important water sources were polluted by dead cattle. Panicking creditors called in outstanding loans. On some overgrazed ranges, experienced stockmen thought it would take ten or fifteen acres to yield what one acre yielded in 1870. Those who survived knew they must implement improved husbandry practices.

TROUBLE BREWING ON THE RANGE

If they weathered the Great Die Up, ranchers knew they had to restructure. They examined better range management practices, including reducing cattle numbers, cutting hay for winter, developing water sources, and implementing better winter ranges.

But curiously, restructuring also meant exacting a tighter control over their land, especially checking the *rustling problems*. Rustling problems certainly meant cattle theft, but specifically it became the catchall term for stemming the flood of homesteaders, as well as reclaiming land set-tlers had taken.

It was a battle in every sense of the word and on every level. Ranchers used a multipronged attack: restricting brand registration, using tighter regulations on who could be a member of the stock association, control-ling roundups, and giving no quarter—even to legal claims. Furthermore, employees who worked for association ranches were not allowed to own cattle or have a brand. The assumption was a cowboy was paid so little, he had rustled to start a herd and would continue to rustle in the future to build it.

The association also lobbied for protective laws and stricter enforce-ment of existing laws. Two examples were the controversial First and Sec-ond Maverick Laws. Traditionally a "maverick" was an unbranded animal, excluding a calf with its branded mother. Legally, on open range, a maver-ick didn't belong to anyone and could be branded by someone with a reg-istered brand. During the spring roundup, ranchers would separate their cattle and brand their calves. The first controversial Maverick Law made cattle without a brand the exclusive property of the association. It was a carte blanche for cattle bosses to legally take cattle without reciproc-ity. As competition for public land became an issue, large ranches would "ride herd" over homesteaders, taking not only unbranded calves but also confiscating an entire herd. The First Maverick Law not only increased a wealthy "association rancher's" bottom line, it was also an excellent way to keep smaller ranchers from using public land. They feared their cattle would be taken.

The Second Maverick Law gave the Wyoming Livestock Commission—for practical purposes an extension of the Wyoming Stock Growers Asso-ciation—legal authority to impound cattle or herds they "suspected" might be rustled. It was a legal form of theft and intimidation. Even more damag-ing, possessing a bill of sale wasn't necessarily proof of ownership.

Before the Great Die Up, large cattlemen and the Wyoming Stock Growers Association had effectively used range detectives. This would continue, but they would empower such men to use any lethal action to protect their interests. Lynching was an object lesson. When Albert Bothwell learned Ella Watson filed on bottomland with water rights, property he considered his by prior usage, he was livid. Watson and her husband also had fields he needed for winter hay. He couldn't scare her nor would she sell. With six men, he did the unthinkable: He lynched the couple. To publicly justify his actions, hanging a woman was serious business, the association bought editors Ed Towse of the *Cheyenne Sun* and E. A. Slack of the *Cheyenne Daily Leader* to reconstruct her narrative. They spun Watson as "Cattle Kate," the rustler and whore who had to be stopped. The association had the money to make witnesses for the prosecution disappear or turn up dead. It didn't hurt, either, that several cattlemen served on the grand jury.

Both sides played deadly games. George Henderson, the range detective instrumental in the Watson lynching, was killed near the Sweetwater River in 1890, and there were other retaliatory murders. Tom Waggoner was lynched on June 4, 1891. It was two weeks before his body was discovered, and when they found him, the rope had stretched so his feet were touching the ground. *The Newcastle Journal* reported, "The rope had cut through the flesh after it became rotten, and maggots held high carnival over the lifeless body." Later, a range detective named Tom Smith was charged with the murder, but influential men got him released.

NORTHERN WYOMING FARMERS AND STOCK GROWERS ASSOCIATION

Smaller ranchers and homesteaders boldly united to protect their rights, forming the Northern Wyoming Farmers and Stock Growers Association (NWFSGA). They elected the charismatic Nathan Champion as their leader. Naturally this infuriated the Wyoming Stock Growers Association; it was a public slap in their face. They considered this an act of open defiance. Equally brazen, they dared to schedule an unauthorized roundup before the Wyoming Stock Growers Association roundup, which was a violation of the First Maverick Law (unbranded cattle belonged to the Wyoming Stock Growers Association).

Champion was a dynamic, hardworking cowboy who wouldn't knuckle under to threats. He'd also been a trail boss and a foreman. Originally from Round Rock, Texas, he had cattle in his blood. He and his twin brother, Dudley, then cowboyed a herd of longhorns up the

Goodnight-Loving Trail to Wyoming in 1881. They liked the country, so they stayed. First, they worked as cowboys for the big outfits, but it seemed they had dreams of owning their own ranches, dreams that didn't sit well with the stockmen they had worked for. Both were top hands, but both would be murdered. Nate formed his own outfit on the Crazy Woman, a fork of the Powder River, running two hundred head of cattle.

HIRING TEXAS GUNMEN

By early in spring 1892, the cattlemen knew they had to take back their range or risk losing it; drastic times meant drastic actions. Over expensive drinks and fine cigars at the Cheyenne Social Club, they held a council of war. Each man ponied up $1,000 for the war chest. They decided to hire a private army, an expeditionary force to crush the NWFSGA and quell this budding insurrection.

They sent a man to Paris, Texas, to hire Texas gunmen for $5 a day. The association, of course, would also pick up the tab for transportation, food, liquor, and lodging. As an added incentive, the Texans would get a $50 bonus for every rustler they killed. The association would provide a $3,000 life insurance policy, and each man would be gifted a new Colt .45 and a Winchester rifle. Incidentally, $5 per day was a good wage because a working cowboy *might* earn $35 to $40 per month. Late in the nineteenth century, "Texas gunmen" were feared, a fact not lost on the association. In our current cultural mythology, movies, television, and novels, we have come to think of cowboys as gunmen. This is not accurate. In the West, a cowboy or a rancher owning a gun didn't make him a gunfighter. Charles Goodnight observed, "few cowboys became very good with a revolver. Many preferred . . . rifles and shotguns." Granville Stuart, a contemporary who lived in Montana wrote, "Not more than 10 out of 100 cowboys owned a revolver . . . although most of them had a rifle."

CREATING A BLACKLIST

The stockmen's next order of business was easier: creating a blacklist (sometimes called the Death list or a Daisy list). What men did they need to murder? Nathan Champion's name would be at the top. There wasn't much question about who to ramrod the Texans but another Texan, Frank

Canton—a bloody man for a bloody job. He was their most effective cattle detective, and someone they trusted. Perhaps they didn't know, or care, his real name was Josiah Horner. He'd been a cowboy, rustler, and a bank robber. He'd evaded the Texas Rangers and was wanted for murder. Historian Harry Sinclair Drago in *The Great Range Wars: Violence on the Grasslands*, suggested, "Frank Canton was a merciless, congenital, emotionless killer. For pay, he murdered eight—very likely ten men." Canton would go on to have a successful career in law enforcement, including a hitch with Hanging Judge Parker as a US marshal.

THE TEXAS GUNMEN MOVE NORTH

After the Texas gunmen arrived in Casper, Wyoming, they were whisked off to the TTT Ranch. They were joined by range detectives, local gunmen, and political officials. Major Frank Wolcott was in charge, representing the Wyoming Stock Growers Association. Included in this cavalcade were two newspaper reporters, Sam Clover from the *Chicago Herald* and Ed Towse from the *Cheyenne Sun*. The stockmen knew how important it was to have their narrative covered correctly.

Depending on the element of surprise, telegraph wires were cut, and, with accompanying supply wagons, the gunman rode north. They planned to move swiftly; however, they had not planned for muddy spring roads or broken-down wagons. The gunmen, led by Canton, decided to move forward, leaving the wagons to catch up. The bonuses paid for dead rustlers were a powerful incentive.

SHOOT-OUT AT KC RANCH

The Texans, called Invaders by the people in Johnson County, were riding to Buffalo, Wyoming, on a bloody errand. They intended to kill the influential Sheriff Red Angus, among other seditious "rustlers." However, when scout Mike Shonsey met the Invaders en route, he reported that Champion, number one on the blacklist, was at the nearby KC Ranch. With him was ranch hand Ruben "Nick" Ray and two itinerate trappers, Bill Walker and Ben Jones, who had been invited to stay the night. Killing Champion would be the grand prize. His death, the stockmen felt, might unravel the NWFSGA. It would also solve another immediate problem.

If Champion was dead, he couldn't testify against Joe Elliott. Stockmen were justifiably concerned Elliott would implicate prominent cattlemen and Canton to receive a lighter sentence.

Shonsey assumed the four would be playing cards and drinking. Maybe the four would be groggy in the morning and easier to surprise if they were slightly hungover. As Canton knew from firsthand experience, Champion would be difficult to kill. The two trappers would be left unharmed, if possible. Champion and Ray would be left alive if the opportunity presented itself and then ignobly lynched.

Little did the Texans know, this shoot-out at the KC Ranch would become a rallying call, as well as a famous gunfight. It was never intended to be an up-front honor contest, like the O.K. Corral, gunplay lasting less than thirty seconds. The Invaders were paid to kill, not to grandstand or to be killed. A corpse was a bounty, and it didn't matter if the bullet came from the front or the back.

The invaders arrived at the KC well after dark on Friday April 8, 1892, and were strategically positioned around the cabin before dawn. It was a cold, snowy night.

The next day, the gunmen were eager to get the job done and earn the bounty. In the morning when Bill Jones stepped out, he was captured and tied up. Shortly thereafter, Walker, too, was taken without incident. The plan had not changed. When Nick Ray stepped out, "Texas Kid" Tucker, a trigger-happy seventeen-year-old gunman, fired. Ray dropped, sustaining a bad leg wound. Other gunmen opened fire. Champion intuitively reached for his rifle, carefully moving to the side of the door. He returned fire at the barn. Quick as a cat, he retreated and was followed by a barrage of bullets pelting the cabin walls and making hollow smacks. Reloading, he slipped to the door again, firing as fast as he could at the barn and creek bank. There was a slight hesitation in the return fire, enough that Champion swept down and retrieved Ray, dragging him into the cabin. The Texas Kid reportedly shouted, "By God he may be a rustler, but he is a man with guts!"

More bullets battered the walls. Champion was safe for a while, but his situation was grave. Carefully, he moved the injured Ray to the bed. He tried to make him comfortable, plugging the wound the best way he could. Constantly watchful, he fired at every movement or shadow. His biggest worry was they'd rush at him at once. Champion wrote in the notebook he kept in his shirt pocket. He was certain he wasn't going to get out alive, but he refused to give up. In short, tight sentences, Champion penned his thoughts, addressing his words to "The Boys." He wanted his friends to know what had happened. "Me and Nick [Ray] was getting breakfast when the attack took place. There was two men with us—Bill Jones and another man. . . . Boys, there's bullets coming in like hail."

"Nick is shot but not dead. He is awful sick. I must go and wait on him. It's been a bad two hours since the first shot." He knew when the shock wore off that Ray would be in a lot of pain. Champion had to be careful how he moved and stayed in the shadows. A little later he wrote, "Nick is dead. He died about 9 o'clock." "Boys," he wrote as the situation was nearly overwhelming, "I'm feeling pretty lonesome right now. I wish there was someone with me so we could watch all sides at once." If they came, he might get one or two if he was lucky. "It don't look as if there is much show of my getting away."

Later, when he "heard them splitting wood," he knew it wasn't for cooking. They were "going to fire" the cabin. "I think I will make a break when night comes, if alive. Shooting again." In the afternoon, a wagon appeared on the road not far from his cabin. As it approached, the gunmen peppered more shots at the cabin to keep him pinned down. The man in the wagon happened to be his neighbor, Jack Flagg, accompanied by his stepson on horseback. Champion saw a group of men on the road signaling him to stop. Had the Invaders recognized it was Flagg, they would have shot and collected the bounty because Flagg's name was on the Death List, too. Flagg obviously knew something was wrong, but he did not know what he could do against that many hired gunmen. He ordered his team to gallop, probably saving his life. Men scrambled to avoid being hit by the wagon, which gave Flagg the extra seconds he needed. Then a bullet killed one of his horses. He managed to stop the wagon on the middle of the bridge over the Crazy Woman River. Dodging bullets, he cut the remaining horse free and rode away bareback. He raced to tell the ranchers about the gunmen at the KC.

Flagg's wagon effectively blocked the bridge, so the riders following him would have to go downstream to cross. But now the Texans had a better plan. They'd kill Flagg later. In his wagon were flammable pitchy-pine fence posts and hay. Lighting the wagon on fire, they would push it next to the cabin.

"It's not night yet," Champion wrote, but he could see what they were planning. Not long afterward, he penned his last entry, "The house is all fired. Goodbye boys, if I never see you again." He signed his name and buttoned the book in his pocket. The fire was raging, and the roof could collapse at any moment, but he planned to use the smoke as cover. He removed his boots, and with a revolver and rifle, he ran for his life. Naturally, there are different accounts of his death: Champion got a few steps out the door and was immediately shot in the chest, as he fell, he took twenty-four more bullets. Champion burst out of the bin by the side of the house sprinting for the river. In the smoky haze, the riflemen missed. He ran one hundred yards and made the creek bank, but six Texans hidden in the ravine fired as he lifted his Winchester. His shot went wild as a bullet shattered his arm. A second slug punched him in the chest—as he fell, almost in slow motion, twenty-eight more bullets hit him. He died with his clear blue eyes staring at the sky. One of the killers was supposed to have mumbled something like, "He came out fighting and died game."

Canton put a sign on his body, "CATTLE THIEVES BEWARE!"

The Texans had killed Nate Champion, but they'd forfeited the element of surprise. Making a raid on Buffalo was no longer advisable because spies reported Sheriff Red Angus was gathering a posse of at least two hundred men. Over the objection of Frank Canton, who knew better than to let his force get pinned down, Major Walcott ordered a retreat to the TA Ranch not far away. The ranch compound was well situated, having been built on a bend of the river. After they arrived at the ranch, the gunmen drilled additional shooting ports, fortified the cabin, and dug rifle pits.

SHOOT-OUT AT THE TA RANCH

A two-day siege began on Monday, April 11. Red and his posse were brave but not stupid; they weren't about to lose men storming fifty rifles. One of the reporters embedded with the Invaders noted their impatience because being bottled up made the Texans nervous. Several times they

171

tried to escape. Once after a fusillade from every Invader gun, twenty Texans made a wild break but were driven back by posse rifles. The reporter assumed three to five men had been killed. Time was not on the Invaders' side, and to make matters grimmer, the posse had captured the Invaders' supplies. On the brighter side, slippery Mike Shonsey escaped. But because the telegraph wires had been cut, he had to ride a hundred miles to find a working telegraph.

At the ranch, the posse took a cue from the Invaders, but burning wasn't enough. They were going to blow it to hell. The men felled trees, constructing a bulletproof breastwork they attached to the front of a captured wagon. They called it the Arc of Safety. It would protect them as they pushed the wagon close enough to lob sticks of dynamite.

Late in the evening of April 12, President William Henry Harrison received a frantic message from the Governor of Wyoming:

> *About sixty-one owners of livestock are reported to have made an armed expedition into Johnson County for the purpose of protecting their livestock and preventing unlawful roundup by rustlers. They are at 'T.A.' Ranch, thirteen miles from Fort McKinney, and are besieged by Sheriff and posse and by rustlers from that section of the country, said to be two or three hundred in number. The wagons of stockmen were captured and taken away from them and it is reported a battle took place yesterday, during which a number of men were killed. Great excitement prevails. Both parties are very determined and it is feared that if successful will show no mercy to the persons captured. The civil authorities are unable to prevent violence. The situation is serious and immediate assistance will probably prevent great loss of life.*

The president ordered the Secretary of War, Stephen Elkins, to call out the cavalry. His justification was "Protection from invasion and domestic violence," Article IV, Section 4, Clause 2.

Under orders from the president, the United States Sixth Cavalry left Fort McKinney around 2 a.m. on Wednesday, April 13. They were led by Colonel J. J. Van Horn. Their job was to take the gunmen into custody and prevent bloodshed. Van Horn appreciated how tenuous this situation was.

At daybreak, the Arc of Safety was ready to roll into action. According to a firsthand witness, they were within half an hour of blowing the TA cabin and the Texas boys to hell. However, at 6:45 a.m., their plans were disrupted when the Sixth Cavalry showed up. The colonel convinced Sheriff Angus the wisest plan was to have the gunmen surrender to the US army. The soldiers took the Invaders into custody, turning the gunmen over to the legal system. Unsurprisingly, some of the cowboys in the posse were disappointed they didn't get to use the dynamite. The Invaders, on the other hand, were reportedly eager to surrender to the army. They understood there was a high likelihood most of them would have been killed. The army took forty-six men into custody, confiscating five thousand rounds of ammunition, forty-one handguns, and forty-five rifles.

INVADERS PLACED UNDER HOUSE ARREST

The prisoners were taken to Fort McKinney, but an army general decided to move the gunmen to a safer location, arguing there were angry mobs threatening to storm the fort. Johnson County prosecutors objected, but the men were moved to Cheyenne "for their own safety." The association argued, "they could not get a fair trial in Johnson County." As the prosecutors feared, the political and legal tentacles of the Wyoming Stock Growers Association impeded their efforts. None of the cattlemen were charged, but because there wasn't enough room at the jail, the Invaders were taken to Fort Russell and put under "house arrest." The gunmen had to report to their cells each evening.

The Johnson County legal team obtained damaging evidence from Frank Canton's "gripe case," which is now known as a briefcase. Along with a few personal items, there was an incriminatory copy of the Death List. This was big news. *The New York Times* reported on April 23, 1892, "[it] implicates more than twenty prominent stockmen of Cheyenne whose names have not been mentioned heretofore, also several wealthy stockmen of Omaha, as well as to compromise men high in authority in the State of Wyoming. They will all be charged with aiding and abetting the invasion, and warrants will be issued for the arrest of all of them."

But justice was not served. Johnson County was poor. It was swiftly mired in legal technicalities and financial issues, including an $18,000 bill

Johnson County War Invaders, taken May 1892 according to the Wyoming State Library. WYOMING STATE LIBRARY.

from Fort Russell for detaining the prisoners. Johnson County didn't have the money to proceed in a timely fashion, so they were forced to release the gunmen on bail. The bail, naturally, was paid by the cattle barons.

WHO WON?

With no closure, the end seemed unsatisfactory. None of the Invaders were brought to justice, both sides harbored a great deal of anger, and killings continued. A marshal who sided with the Invaders was ambushed, and Mike Shonsey killed Nate Champion's brother, Dudley. He claimed self-defense. Range detectives murdered several men they said were rustlers.

The year 1892 marked the end of open range, and the cattle barons were the losers; they forfeited their monopoly. Change occurred slowly and by degrees. Owners of small ranches gained a voice that was heard locally and nationally. It was, at best, a fragile peace.

15

THREE DAKOTA INDIANS LYNCHED

AN IRATE MOB AVENGES THE SPICER FAMILY

I hate all white people. You are thieves and liars. You have taken away
our lands and made us outcasts.
> —Sitting Bull, speaking in his own language, to a
> standing ovation in 1883. He was a guest speaker at the
> ceremony that opened the Northern Pacific Railroad.
> His interpreter translated his words as, "I'm pleased to
> be here—I look forward to peace and prosperity."

WILLIAMSPORT, NORTH DAKOTA, 1897

In 1897, three Sioux Indians were incarcerated at the Williams County
Jail in North Dakota. Alec Caudotte had been convicted of first-degree
murder. Paul Holy Track and Philip Ireland, two teenagers, had admitted they were accessories to the brutal slaying of the Spicer family. There
were rumors the killers might escape. To protect the community, the
sheriff placed a twenty-four-hour guard at the jail. The community was
pleased Caudotte and the other two would face charges. However, when
the North Dakota Supreme Court granted Caudotte a new trial, there
was a fear the killer might go free. Apparently the court felt the prosecution needed more evidence, even though there were six dead Spicer
bodies to account for. It was rumored Caudotte admitted his guilt and
had attempted suicide. Wasn't that proof of guilt? Some of the ranchers
and businessmen were not satisfied because this was a matter of public

safety. They had a duty to protect the community if the law would not. At 2 a.m. on a chilly November evening, forty men rode into Williamsport and quietly tied their horses near the jail. Deputy Tom Kelly was on guard duty, playing solitaire to pass the time. He half expected a few friends to drop in after the lodge meeting. They might bring him a drink and something to eat. When he heard a knock on the door, he was not surprised. He wasn't worried about someone breaking into the jail; rather, his job was to keep the prisoners from breaking out. When he opened the door, a group of masked men crowded him. Suddenly, the business end of a Colt was thrust in his face. A voice told him to unlock the cells holding the murdering Indians. Some of the vigilantes were carrying ropes. Their intention was obvious. Deputy Kelly put up a semblance of resistance but had no choice. After more prodding, he yielded.

Hemp ropes were placed around the necks of the prisoners. The three were told they needed to prepare to die. There was no need to be gentle. They drug the men out and took them to what is called a "beef windlass." It was constructed of two sturdy logs standing up in the ground with a log laying across the top of them. The crossbar of the lass was used to hang beef carcasses for butchering. With the nooses cinched around their necks, their hands and feet were tied, and the ends of the ropes were thrown over the bar. They slowly pulled the rope until the killers were dangling in the air. Once the deed was done, the vigilantes rode off into the night. The saying was "the only good Indian was a dead Indian"—or better yet, three dead Indians. The bodies hung until the next evening. No one bothered to cut them down.

A triple hanging made the headlines. The *Sacramento Daily Union*, of November 15, 1897, read: "Murderer of the Spicer Family Strung. A Half Breed and Two Full Bloods Pay the Penalty." Other newspapers headlines blurted out:

MOB LAW IN NORTH DAKOTA. Three Indians Lynched for the Murder of Six Members of the Spicer Family.

THE COURTS WERE TOO SLOW. The Alleged Ringleader of the Murderers had obtained a New Trial After Having Been Sentenced to Death.

EMMONS COUNTY HISTORICAL SOCIETY COLLECTION
November 14, 1897 Williamsport, N.D.
Lynching of Alec Caudotte, Phillip Ireland, &
Paul Holy Track

North Dakota Historical Society/Emmons County Historical Society Collection
Photo Number: 00281-00038.

THE LYNCHING WAS COOLLY PLANNED. The Lynching
Was Carried Off Without a Break.

THE SIOUX HANGING IN 1862

Of course, these three were not the first or the last Sioux Indians to
be hanged. The most famous hanging occurred on December 26, 1862.
Thirty-eight were hanged simultaneously. As a point of interest, this was
the largest group hanging historically recorded in the United States.
Three hundred Sioux Indians were found guilty and sentenced to the
gallows, but President Abraham Lincoln commuted all the sentences
excepting for those who were executed. In July 1862, greedy officials and

177

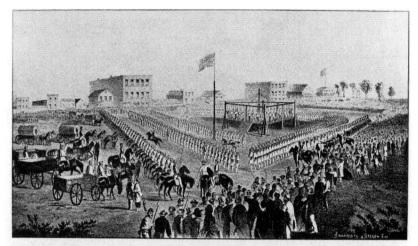

The hanging of thirty-eight Sioux Indians at Mankato, Minn., December 26th, 1862. The three story building in left front with the low shed lying between it and the next building on the right, formed the prison where the three hundred condemned Indians were confined during the winter of 1862-3.

Hanging of 38 Sioux Indians at Mamkato, Minnesota, December 26, 1862.
WELLCOME LIBRARY, LONDON. WELLCOME IMAGES IMAGES@WELLCOME.AC.UK HTTP://WELL-COMEIMAGES.ORG COPYRIGHTED WORK AVAILABLE UNDER CREATIVE COMMONS ATTRIBUTION ONLY LICENSE CC BY 4.0 HTTP://CREATIVECOMMONS.ORG/LICENSES/BY/4.0/.

Indian agents had withheld promised Sioux Indian gratuities until "official" and "unofficial" bribes were paid in full. As a result, the Santee Sioux Indians were quite literally starving. They were displeased and angered by their displacement to a small reservation and being barred from hunting or gathering food in the traditional manner. Eventually, they went on the warpath, killing white settlers and taking prisoners. In the Battle at Birch Coulee, on September 2, 1862, thirteen US soldiers were killed and forty wounded. It wasn't until the Battle of Wood Lake in September of that year that the warriors were defeated.

THE BLIND PIG

When North Dakota gained statehood, its constitution banned saloons. This law put a damper on business but didn't stop saloons from operating. They went "underground." Such illegal saloons were called "blind pigs," and those who operated them were called "piggers." On February 14, 1897, Frank Blackhawk and Alec Caudotte tried to buy alcohol at a blind pig. It had long been a criminal offense to sell alcohol to Indians, but it occurred frequently. However, piggers had to be a bit more cautious because the saloon prohibition was in place. Allegedly the pigger told the two he was temporarily out of alcohol, but he said a local man named Pepper might be able to accommodate them.

Boldly the two went to Pepper's home and asked him where he kept his liquor hidden and if they could buy some. It's not plausible that Pepper would tell the two where his alcohol was stored. Similarly, like the pigger, Pepper probably recognized this wasn't a risk-free sale. Jokingly, Pepper told Blackhawk and Caudotte his booze was hidden in Thomas Spicer's basement. The Spicers were a religious family; Thomas Spicer was a minister and preacher. His basement would be the last place in the county where alcohol, especially illegal alcohol, would be stored. Neither Blackhawk or Caudotte caught the sarcasm, however, nor did they recognize that this man was putting them off. Attempting to defuse the situation, he said something he thought was humorous. One may surmise the two took Pepper literally. Pepper likely had a few laughs at their expense while he shared this comical anecdote with his drinking buddies that evening. English was not Blackhawk's nor Caudotte's first language, and this was not the first or last time there had been critical miscommunication between two dissimilar cultures.

THE SPICER FAMILY MURDERS

A few days later, on February 17, 1897, Blackhawk and Caudotte decided to call on the Spicers. They brought along George Defender and two teens, Paul Holy Track and Philip Ireland. It appears from court testimony the robbery was planned in advance. Perhaps they had also planned to use deadly force if Thomas Spicer did not cooperate. It seems unlikely that five young men would take a shotgun to someone's home to buy alcohol otherwise. Pepper had told them the alcohol was in the Spicer basement, and they took him literally. When they talked to Spicer, it appears to have been a one-sided discussion. He kept trying to explain he didn't know what they were talking about. And, no, he didn't have alcohol in his basement. The five were frustrated and angry.

At some point one of them shot Spicer in the back with the shotgun. After blowing a large, gory hole in his back, they disfigured him with an axe. One of them went to the house and got Spicer's wife. When she stepped into the barn, they discharged the second barrel. The five then headed to the house. On discovering Mrs. Spicer's elderly mother, they beat her to death with a blunt instrument. Meanwhile Mrs. Rowse, their married daughter who was visiting her parents while her husband was away, locked herself in a bedroom with her twin boys, Alvin and Albert. They were eighteen months old. Apparently, Caudotte broke in, but Mrs. Rowse repelled his efforts with the butt or barrel of a shotgun. The fact that she didn't fire the weapon leads us to assume it was not loaded. Then Paul Holy Track broke in. According to court records, Mrs. Rowse hit him with the blade from a hoe; there was no handle. Her blow hit Holy Track's hat brim and then smacked his face, cutting his hat and wounding him. Mrs. Rowse was overpowered and beaten to death with a broken piano leg. After this, the murderers bludgeoned the toddlers.

THE TRIAL

On February 20, 1897, news about the Spicer murders reached the authorities. The state attorney visited the site as law enforcement began their investigation of the crime. Holy Track and Ireland were questioned and arrested. From there, the record gets fuzzy. They confessed, which led to the arrest of the other three. Later their stories shifted, but Holy Track and Ireland were still vital to the prosecutor's case. At the outset they testified Blackhawk planned the incident and Caudotte committed the murders. Later they said they all participated in the killing.

Caudotte was tried first at the Williamsport courthouse with an all-white jury. Judge Walter Winchester was presiding. Much of Caudotte's testimony was translated into English by an interpreter. He was found guilty of first-degree murder. The jury recommended hanging. At this point the defense asked for a new trial, but the judge denied it.

George Defender's defense team requested a new judge. Otto Sawter replaced Judge Winchester. Shocking much of the community, Defender's trial ended with a hung jury after sixty hours of deliberation. A new trial was necessary. Even more astonishing, Caudotte's conviction had been successfully appealed. The North Dakota Supreme Court granted a new trial for Caudotte. The testimony of Holy Track and Ireland was not enough to convict him. To sustain a conviction, the Supreme Court ruled there needed to be more evidence.

This was troubling news. The court system had failed not only the Spicer family, but it also had failed the good citizens who trusted that justice would be served. If these self-confessed murderers went free, what would happen? The answer was plain enough: frontier justice. Caudotte, Holy Track, and Ireland were being held at the Williamsport jail. The other two were at a Bismarck jail. By no means could these "Indian killers" go free. Forty men, good and true, saddled up on Saturday evening to balance the scales. They came with sidearms, rifles, and plenty of rope.

The charges against the other two men were dropped. Defender died of tuberculosis before the new century. Blackhawk lived until 1926.

What is noteworthy is that due process was observed. There wasn't enough evidence to convict American Indians in a white court with a white jury, and no one in the lynch mob was brought to justice.

Massacre at Wounded Knee Ghost Dance: Congress Bans All American Indian Dances

Religious tolerance has always been a complicated issue. In 1883, the US Congress passed what was called the Code of Indian Offenses. Its purpose was to help American Indians assimilate into the white culture. Any practice that identified cultural or religious practices was prohibited. As part of this law, the Courts of Indian Offenses and a tribal police force were also created. This meant that medicine men and women could no longer, legally, practice their callings and potlatches were illegal. Most offensive, at least for the Lakota, was the banning of the Sun Dance and the Ghost Dance. This law empowered federal agents to withhold food and gratuities if tribal members refused to capitulate, or if they continued to engage in "subversive or immoral" behaviors, the Indian agent could use whatever force he deemed necessary.

By 1890, the different western tribes were subdued, and the majority were living on reservations. A new millenarian movement, however, was sweeping through the northern tribes; it offered hope to a defeated people. The Prophet of the Paiute Indians, Wovoka (Jack Wilson), taught the doctrine of the Ghost Dance. He prophesied a golden era of peace and prosperity, as well as the return of the buffalo herd, and the end of Americans encroachment on tribal lands. He said if American Indians united together in the Ghost Dance, they would be able to join with the spirits of their dead and usher in a thousand-year utopia. As the movement spread, each tribe practiced variations according to their own beliefs and rituals. Naturally, federal agents and officials did their best to break up this movement, especially the dances. According to one report, thirty reservations had been infected by the "Indian Messiah" craze. If enforcement wasn't quickly dispatched, much of the assimilation the government had established would have been in vain. It was not acceptable to allow the tribes to think they were Indians again, hoping for the "Red Second Coming." Many Lakota embraced the movement enthusiastically, incorporating elements of the Sun Dance Ceremony. Men, women, and children would form a circle, join hands, and move clockwise around a small cottonwood tree they placed in the center. They left tokens—ribbons, cloth, American flags—on the branches for the spirits of the dead. There would be a prayer and chants followed by the beating of drums. Then dancers would get up and dance alone as they felt directed. Into their Ghost Dance, the Lakota incorporated

The Ghost Dance by the Oglala Lakota Sioux at Pine Ridge Agency. Drawn by Frederic Remington from sketches taken on the spot. Illustrated in *Harper's Weekly*, December 6 1890, p. 960–61. COURTESY OF LIBRARY OF CONGRESS

the Ghost Shirt. It was a shirt made of buckskin, but it was bestowed with spiritual powers that would stop a bullet. On December 15, 1890, soldiers came to arrest Sitting Bull. The Indian agent at Standing Rock Reservation disliked him and felt he needed to be removed because he was stirring up contention. When he was taken into custody by Indian police, his men were upset and opened fire. The Indian police returned fire and murdered Sitting Bull, shooting him in the chest and face. Upon hearing the news of Sitting Bull's death, a band of Miniconjou Lakota fled from their agency. They feared reprisal. They camped in a place called Wounded Knee. On December 28, 1890, however, Colonel James Forsyth and his troops had surrounded them. The following day, the leader, Big Foot, told Forsyth they would surrender. On December 29, 1890, US troops arrived to disarm the Indians. However, as soldiers searched the lodges they discovered hidden weapons. Later when several troopers disarmed a man who was deaf, his weapon discharged. The situation became tense. Several men started dancing the Ghost Dance. They encouraged the others to join in and put on their Ghost Shirts, rendering the soldiers' bullets harmless. Three hundred Lakota men, women, and children were killed by four Hotchkiss guns that fired sixty rounds a minute and the soldiers' rifles. It was called the Battle of Wounded Knee, but it was not a battle, it was a massacre.

16

BROWN'S PARK

RANGE WAR FOR A MOUNTAIN VALLEY ON THE UTAH-COLORADO BORDER

Raiders then wasn't bothered by the idea they was doing wrong. They looked upon the cattle kings as range hogs having no legitimate right to their kingdoms and cattle they had grabbed, and they looked upon the cattle as legitimate spoils of war.
—Matt Warner, *Last of the Bandit Raiders*

UTAH-COLORADO-WYOMING BORDER, 1900

Orah Ben Haley owned the Two Bar ranch, but he wanted more. His ranching interests in Wyoming and Colorado were vast. He controlled sixty thousand acres. Haley had his eye on Brown's Park, a mountain valley six miles wide and thirty-five miles long, with the Green River running down the middle. This acquisition was the next move in building his cattle empire. Unlike previous conflicts where cattlemen fought to keep homesteaders off open range, which was public land, Haley was clearly stepping over the line. Brown's Park was crisscrossed with small ranches, many having been there for some time. He would take Brown's Park because he could; nickel-and-dime ranchers didn't know how to fully use the land. Haley was accustomed to getting what he wanted. He had armed riders, cowboys, investment capital, and the law on his side. Like a feudal lord, if you were strong enough to take it, you did. This overlooked valley would be the crown jewel in his ranching kingdom.

He started moving in Two Bar cattle, sweeping up smaller herds in his way. Any rancher who fought him would be considered an outlaw and treated as such. Conversely, the small ranches he tried to intimidate considered Two Bar cattle fair game. Haley had dealt the first hand in what would be called the Brown's Park Range War. He wasn't pleased that his cattle were considered spoils of war for midnight riders bold enough to bolster their own herds; neither did they seem to fret about taking a side of beef for the kitchen table. They said, "We thank God for our bread and Ora Ben Haley for our meat." But Haley had other moves up his sleeve. He hired a range detective who wasn't afraid to pull the trigger. There were two men who had been especially bold, and it was time for Matt Rash and Isom Dart to pay for their sins. If they could not be scared off, they must be killed. Haley knew a man with a system that wouldn't fail.

BROWN'S PARK

Tom Horn fixed rustling problems. He had a new .30-30 rifle and knew how to use it. He also had a knack for killing rustlers while he was "someplace else," giving himself plausible deniability. Horn would shoot his man from a safe, comfortable distance, and then he would leave a conspicuous calling card, an empty cartridge or a stone under the dead man's head.

Horn would slip into Brown's Park under cover, as a drifter named Jim Hicks. He was the kind of man who didn't mind getting to know a fellow before he killed him. Horn said it was his way of making sure he only punished those who were truly guilty.

Haley didn't know it, but he was in for a fight. In the end, it would be a battle he would not win. The men and women in Brown's Park were seasoned Westerners who knew how to use guns and play rough. They would not be bullied like the homesteaders he was used to dealing with.

While many honest men and women made a living off the land in Brown's Park, it was remote and isolated. It was similar to Robber's Roost or Hole-in-the-Wall. In Western mythology, it was said that Brown's Park welcomed honest ranchers, outlaws, rustlers, and gunmen, whereas sheriffs, marshals, deputies, range detectives, and cattle barons entered at their own risk. Most of the Wild Bunch, including Butch Cassidy,

Sundance Kid, Matt Warner, and Elza Lay, found it a safe place to hide between jobs. It was a neutral zone where local ranchers didn't ask questions and outlaws were polite, helping with ranch work and chores. It was said that outlaws occasionally enjoyed doing a bit of rustling to help pay their keep.

In Western legends, the outlaws had a code for sanctuaries like Brown's Park: Be good to the folks, pay too much for what you bought, and stay away from local women. In return, the local people would be good to you. What happened somewhere else was not their business. Men on the run could get resupplied, trade horses, or sell questionable stock. They were able to socialize and go to barn dances and to picnics.

Brown's Park was also called Brown's Hole. Hole was a word the mountain men used for a valley. An example is Jackson's Hole in Wyoming. The Ute and Shoshone Indian nations had lived in the area for hundreds of years. In 1825, William Ashley rode through, and a couple of years later Kit Carson trapped the area. It was named after a mountain man named Baptiste Brown. He got snowed in one winter. In 1869, John Wesley Powell floated the Green River and thought it a beautiful place. Texas cowboys had driven cattle and wintered in Brown's Park in the 1870s but didn't stay. There were settlers and mountain men in the Park when Herb and Elizabeth Bassett started their ranch in 1878. Their outfit was mostly run by Elizabeth while Herb ran a school, read, and tended the garden. Elizabeth and her daughters, Ann and Josie Bassett, were famous and were referred to as the Bassett Women. They were personal friends of Butch Cassidy and other outlaws. Josie had a colorful life, marrying many times. In folk legend, she supposedly poisoned one of her husbands. You can see her cabin in Dinosaur National Park, near Vernal, Utah. Ann was called "Queen of the Rustlers" and was supposed to be engaged to Matt Rash before he was shot. Later she would help make a fool of Orah Ben Haley.

MATT RASH

Matt Rash was a dashing Texas cowboy who brought a herd north, fell in love with Brown's Park, and never left. We are not sure about all the details of his murder because accounts vary. What we have pieced together is that he was alive on July 7, 1900, because he stopped at the Bassett ranch. Several days later, July 10, 1900, several teenaged boys rode to his place. They investigated further and found his body. Considering the heat and decomposition, it appears he was shot on July 8, 1900, while eating lunch. The killer stood in the door of his small cabin to shoot. A bullet entered under his arm, the second entered his back, but he had enough strength to crawl to his bunk. For good measure, the killer also shot his favorite horse. Legends say Rash wrote the killer's name with his blood before he died. The story is too good to fade away, but we don't really know. Maybe the murderer carried the dying man to his bed; again, nothing is conclusive. A coroner's inquest was held and Rash was buried next to his cabin.

He was thirty-seven years old and an excellent cowboy who could take care of himself. Reportedly, he'd been warned that unless he left the area he'd be killed for rustling. It was one thing to confront a man head-on, but it was something else to be ambushed while eating lunch. Rash was the head of the Brown's Park Cattlemen Association, a small group of ranchers. He'd been accused of fixing a brand a time or two, but Haley had hired the best.

ISOM DART

Isom Dart was number two on Tom Horn's list. On September 26, 1900, Horn, range detective, had publicly signed a complaint that Dart was a rustler. Dart had a questionable record concerning rustling but was well-thought of in Brown's Hole. It may be that Horn thought after Rash's death, the publicity would be enough to encourage Dart to move on, but it didn't. However, Dart was worried about the threat. This was his home. He'd been born a slave in Arkansas but had proven himself in Texas. Dart was a fine cowboy and stockman. He was also considered one of the best horseback riders in the region and was known for his skill of breaking horses. Dart was supposed to be an artist at doctoring brands. He'd been indicted for rustling but never convicted. He, too, was well liked by the Bassett family. On October 3, 1900, a cool, breezy day, Dart was shot walking out his cabin door. His friends scrambled for cover. Two .30-30 shells were left by a tree where Horn stood as he fired.

Ned Huddleston, aka "Isom Dart," Brown's Hole, Wyoming. PUBLIC DOMAIN/PBS.

AFTERMATH

Orah Ben Haley continued to fight for control of Brown's Park. The bewitching Ann Bassett either seduced Haley's brilliant manager, "Hy" Henry Bernard or, at the least, got him to marry her in 1903. He was quite a bit older. Haley immediately fired Bernard, which was a bad business move. The stormy marriage between Ann and Hy lasted six years. Later, Ann would be arrested for rustling and would make a fool of Haley. During the trial, she exposed his fraudulent behavior, including that he had cheated on his taxes. Haley was forced to sell his holdings and died in 1919.

17

TOM HORN

"KILLING MEN IS MY SPECIALTY. . . . IT'S A BUSINESS PROPOSITION."

I think I have a corner on the market.

—Tom Horn

CHEYENNE, WYOMING, 1903

How did the state of Wyoming kill a killer like Tom Horn? They hung him by the neck until he was dead. It took seventeen minutes for him to die, but by all considerations this was a sloppy hanging.

On a cold morning, the day before his birthday on the November 20, 1903, Tom Horn was hung. He didn't know it, but he'd run out of time before he was arrested for the murder of a fourteen-year-old boy. He was a liability for the prominent men in the Wyoming Stock Growers Association. Maybe he'd done his job too well. Ironically, the murder of Willie Nickell on July 11, 1901, may have been one he didn't commit. His arrest, trial, and execution were front page news. For nearly 120 years, there have been questions about how the prosecution's evidence was collected and whether or not Horn had a fair trial. There is little debate, however, that he was a killer.

We can't know how he really felt on the gallows, but observers said he was more composed than the lawmen assigned to hang him. On the scaffold, he said to Sheriff Edward Smalley, "Ed, that's the sickest looking lot of damned sheriffs I've seen." This was now the new West and it was only proper that a "stock detective," a polite word for a hired killer, go the way of the buffalo, the grizzly bear, and the Plains Indians. After all, the Ford Model A was in production, the Wright Brothers were weeks away from their historical flight at Kitty Hawk, and *The Great Train Robbery*, was showing in theaters. The West had been won, and the new century was full of promise and hope.

The art of hanging, however, even with the newfangled water-powered Julian gallows, apparently wasn't an exact science. A damned, old-fashioned truth was obvious, Horn's neck was not broken properly. We're told he probably didn't suffer. A newspaper man wrote he was knocked cold when the noose's coil whacked his head. Not dying right away, though, made it awkward. The lawmen hoped to get it right the first time. A doctor kept checking his pulse as everyone waited for his heart to stop. Seventeen minutes is a long time when you expect someone to die in the time it takes to swallow. Perhaps the designer, James Julian, should have included instructions. Maybe Sheriff Richard Proctor should have added another foot of rope because a drop of 4½ feet evidently wasn't enough. And yet, as old-timers knew, Horn was a large man, so there was always a danger his head might rip off. As it was, his chest didn't clear the trapdoor. Because technology was the future, Wyoming inventor James Julian saw a need to reduce "hangman's guilt." With water gallows, he explained, execution was more like a suicide. The condemned would step or be placed on the trapdoor, and the person's weight on the trapdoor would pull a stopper from a barrel of water. As the water drained, a float attached to a lever triggered the latch on the trapdoor, dropping the condemned to their death.

Horn's hanging was singularly famous in the West. It was surely the biggest event to hit Cheyenne, Wyoming, since his jury trial. The talk divided the town because many were working folks, homesteaders, and small ranchers, folks who had little sympathy for the heavy-handed escapades of cattle companies or contract killers. Newspapers fueled speculation about jailbreak plots; the wildest was Butch Cassidy and the Wild Bunch rescuing the prisoner. Other plots were uncovered. Once Horn and another prisoner beat up a guard and nearly escaped. Conversely, during his twenty-two-month incarceration, vigilante groups, one fueled by the furious Kels Nickell, father of murdered Willie, wanted to lynch him. Sheriff Smalley wasn't taking any chances. He had the governor send troops and posted a man on the roof with a Gatling gun.

HANGED "UNCONFESSED"

After his appeal was denied and the hanging loomed, the question in southern Wyoming was, would Horn panic at the noose? Would he expose the men who hired him? In the saloons and gambling houses, heavy bets were placed on either side. On the morning of his hanging, Horn wrote letters and ate a large breakfast. He'd not finished his last cigar when deputies came. He left it burning on a grate. It was a short walk to a short service. Everyone knew he was here to die. His friend Charlie Irwin and his brother, Frank, sang a hymn of comfort, "Life's Railway to Heaven." Sheriff Proctor cinched the straps tightly around his chest and legs. The Episcopal minister, Reverend George Rafter, read a church prayer for the dying. Afterward, a concerned Irwin blurted out, "Tom, did you confess to the preacher?"

"No," Horn said.

The sheriff asked if he had any last words. "No," Horn said. His time had run out. The black hood was tied and the noose snugged properly around his neck. He was lifted on the trapdoor. Everyone heard the incongruous gurgling of water rushing out of the barrel. It was taking so long. Through his black hood, Horn commented to the hangman, "What's the matter, getting nervous I might tip over?" There were more anxious sighs. In all, it took exactly thirty-one seconds before he fell. At one point, it was said the shaken Sheriff Smalley was overcome with emotion and buried his head in his arm.

Horn did not get a clean kill.

He died unconfessed before God. He died unconfessed before the law. He died unconfessed before a nervous handful of wealthy Wyoming ranchers at the Cheyenne Social Club. When the news was confirmed— and that he had taken his secrets to his grave—the cattle lords gasped a collective sigh of relief. They surely ordered another round of drinks and

193

Photograph of Tom Horn. PUBLIC DOMAIN/WIKIMEDIA COMMONS.

champagne for all. Tacitly, when Horn was jailed, he had been told if he'd keep his nerve and didn't talk, he'd be freed. In the end, the cattle barons did precious little to vindicate him as they scrambled to restructure what had become a public relations disaster. The exception was his friend, John Coble of the Iron Mountain Ranch Company. Coble stood by Horn until the end. In fact, some say Coble may have paid nearly $10,000 for Horn's defense.

THE WARRIOR'S CODE OF HONOR

One of his defense attorneys, T. Blake Kennedy, was asked fifty years later if he thought Horn murdered Willie Nickell. Kennedy paused and said, "[Tom] killed plenty of other people. I don't know if he shot Willie."

Horn lived by a code, a thwarted one perhaps, but a code, nevertheless. More specifically, it was his version of a warrior's honor code or a "warrior's way." It's tempting to oversimplify, but he may have seen himself as an errant medieval knight following his brand of frontier chivalry. Today we might liken him to a samurai following his bushido. He was certainly influenced by his years in the Apache Wars and by Indigenous warrior societies. Horn, always a restless wanderer, never fit into social constructs for long. Some psychology experts, suggest he displayed some psychopathic behaviors. He wandered the Wild West on his steed, toting a Winchester rifle and a Colt six-gun, looking for a quest, a quasi-boon from feudal lords, in this case the cattle barons. He prided himself on his loyalty, an important part of the warrior's code. On November 17, 1903, three days before his scheduled execution, Horn wrote a letter to his friend and employer, Coble. There was speculation that when the rope was put around Horn's neck, he would "tell all." Horn put up a brave front; however, what is more important, Horn was telling Coble that he would not betray him or the other cattlemen. Horn would take "their" secrets to his grave. This letter was included in his 1904 autobiography, *Life of Tom Horn: Government Scout & Interpreter, Written by Himself*:

> *Dear Johnie:*
> *Proctor [sic] told me that it was all over with me except the applause part of the game.*
> *You know they can't hurt a real Christian, and as I am prepared, it is all right.*
> *I thoroughly appreciate all you have done for me. No one could have done more. Kindly accept my thanks, for if ever a man had a true friend, you have proven yourself one to me.*

Remember me kindly to all my friends, if I have any besides yourself.
. . . I am just the same as ever, and will remain so.
Yours truly,
Tom Horn

As he settled into his career as a cattle detective or murderer for hire, he saw rustlers and homesteaders, sometimes called "nesters," as humans without honor. Killing them was like shooting wolves; you do it any way you can. Because they displayed no honor, he was therefore free to use deception, surprise attack, or long-distance backshooting to accomplish his task. His presence on a range created a reign of terror. He sent public and private threatening letters to suspects, he put stones under a victim's head, or he left spent shells from his ambush point. It was said that mothers would tell their children to be good or Tom Horn would get them. His threats created panic, and many who received them, guilty or not, packed up and left. Horn "claimed" he never used deadly force unless he, himself, found direct evidence of guilt. However, his self-destructive drinking coupled with braggadocio were not like classical eloquent epic boasts; they were more akin to pathological rants.

Glendolene Kimmell was the schoolteacher who befriended Horn. Some have linked the two romantically, including the 1980 movie, *Tom Horn*, starring Steve McQueen. There is no evidence of a romance, however, nor does it fit into a historical chronology. Kimmell, who helped edit and revise *Life of Tom Horn, Government Scout and Interpreter, Written by Himself*, published in 1904, wrote, "Riding hard, drinking hard, fighting hard, so passed his days until he was crushed between the grindstones of two civilizations." Some have been tempted, I think mistakenly, to romanticize his life. It is said he was a man who outlived his time, a fallen everyman in the last act of an Old West morality play. Or, he highlighted the transitions between the old and new, the ending of the frontier and the ushering in of the modern age. It's fair to say Tom Horn represents a kind of liminal space in his time, but more importantly, his story is about a troubled man who turned to the dark side and murdered for money.

With that said, one must not lay all the blame on a saw when an old-growth forest is logged. Horn was guilty of taking lives, but he usually didn't shoot people for the hell of it. He was paid to pull the trigger on his Winchester. It's too easy, maybe too convenient, to place an unfair share of blame on one man, even if he's a convenient lightning rod. If the system was just, or if we wanted to balance that historic scale, a group of wealthy cattlemen should have been on the gallows scaffold with him, nooses on their necks, and black hoods over their faces.

Horn was generally oblivious about how quickly he was straying outside the cattlemen's orbit. Until it was too late, at best, he had only an inkling about how toxic he had become. The high-profile Nickell killing had polarized the political climate. His boisterous drinking binges had become embarrassing. Most of the "good old boys" in the Wyoming Stock Growers Association were more likely to crucify than shield him. Horn was never able to understand that he was not a member of their exclusive club. He was more like a whore they passed around in a dark alley to suit their needs. He could never be acknowledged publicly, particularly under a focused spotlight of legal and social criticism. His professional service had served them, but he was now a bad cultural fit. He was a tool no longer politically fashionable, and they, ironically, didn't want to be guilty by association.

He was a talented tracker and scout, but he was a liar, a braggart, and he killed people for money.

THOMAS HORN JR.

Untangling the *historic* from the *legendary* Tom Horn is a fascinating process, but it can be messy and isn't an exact science. Some of the confusion comes from his autobiography, which is colorful but not factual. The real story—sometimes dark, controversial, and frightening—is worth unpacking from the plethora of "yellow press" journalism during his trial and execution, historical documents, first- and secondhand accounts, pulp fiction and dime novels, television and Hollywood treatments, and unsubstantiated, but well-meaning, historical reports. We know something about him. In the *Denver Post*, Leonel O'Bryan, pseudonym Pry Polly, wrote, that he was slightly taller than six feet, "was 190 pounds, he was not fleshy. His feet were small . . . his hands were brutally coarse, with stubby fingers and long hairs growing down to the knuckles." He had dark gray eyes, and some said "shifty-eyes." He could be quiet if he wasn't drinking, he liked to read, and for his day, with little formal education, he could compose a passable sentence.

Thomas Horn Jr. was born to Thomas S. Horn Sr. and his wife, Mary Ann Miller Horn, on November 21, 1860, in northern Missouri. The Horns farmed six hundred acres. His parents were both strict Campbellites. His father didn't believe in sparing the rod. Tom Jr. loved being outdoors and longed to be free from the drudgery of farm chores. He said he'd watch and daydream about the wagons going West, wishing he was going, too, preferring a life of adventure, hunting, and fishing.

Such idleness, however, for the elder Horn was devilry and was not to be tolerated. He was certain a good caning was the best way to beat the hell out of a child so the light of God might enter. When the young Tom talked back, as he sometimes did, it illustrated how badly he needed further correction and an additional whipping. There was a developing rage in the young boy that would become harder to control. In the middle of eight brothers and sisters, Tom felt he couldn't measure up to his parents' expectations. He found refuge in the stolen hours he spent outdoors.

His fondest memory of Missouri had little to do with his family. It was about his beloved dog, Shedrick or "Shed," considered to be his only friend. In his autobiography, he wrote about a fight he provoked with two migrant boys. They ended up shooting his dog. He brought the body home in a cart and buried him. Nearly thirty years later, when he wrote his autobiography in prison, he tells the reader this was the only "real sorrow of my life." Although it's psychological speculation, which is always hard to quantify, this incident appears to be a kind of emotional watershed. He learned about loss and the finality of relationships. He wrote that he bore the sorrow alone because he didn't know how to share it, likely because of the dissonance in his home. His developing rage and angst were partly assuaged by emotional distancing. A few months later, he had words with his father. If we want to take him at his word, as a fourteen-year-old, he wanted what was called "show," a chance to fight. His father gave him show, and he was hurt so badly he said he couldn't leave the barn until the next day. He said it took a week to heal. He visited the grave of his dog and then ran away.

ARIZONA TERRITORY

Around 1875, according to his autobiography, Horn drifted into the Arizona Territory; biographer Larry Ball, however, in *Tom Horn in Life and Legend*, feels 1881 was more likely. He did odd jobs, worked on the railroad, and as a cowboy picked up a working knowledge of border Spanish. At eighteen he was hired as a packer for the famous Apache Indian scout, Al Sieber. The older man took a liking to him. Horn wrote that he looked up to the gruff old German rather like a surrogate father figure. He became an apprentice civilian scout and would later become chief of scouts for the US army. He lovingly described the rugged old man who apparently carved notches in his weapons for every kill he made. "When I met Al Sieber," Tom wrote, "he carried twenty major knife, lance, arrow and gunshot wounds . . . at the time of his discharge . . . he carried fifty-three knife cuts on the butts and stocks of his various guns."

Horn was always a good outdoorsman, but he became a superb tracker, learning how to live off the land from the Apache Indian scouts. He picked up a working knowledge of the language and worked under Generals George Crook and Nelson Miles. He claimed to be fluent in Spanish and Apache but never was. Horn was in the field during the Geronimo Campaign and went deep into the Sierra Madras in Mexico. He was at the Battle of Cibecue Creek on August 30, 1881, and at the Battle of Big Dry Wash on July 17, 1882. He also was at Geronimo's surrender on September 4, 1886, but unlike his mythology, Geronimo knew who he was, but they were not friends and Horn did not act as interpreter. He served with distinction and was known as a tough man who could "track bees in a blizzard." During the Apache Wars, some historians wonder if Horn started to change, to harden. A Wyoming rancher, Jim King, knew Horn and said, "It was everybody's business to kill at a price . . . the idea soaked and baked into his soul that there was nothing wrong in killing renegades."

He tried ranching in Aravaipa Canyon, Arizona Territory, after scouting but went broke. He wrote in his autobiography it was because of "rustlers." He was in a silver mining venture and was a deputy. He was associated with the Pleasant Valley War, but his participation was sketchy. As an army scout and a rancher, he knew both John Graham and Ed Tewksbury in Pleasant Valley. Later both Sieber and Horace Dunlap felt he did not take a side. Historian Dan L. Thrapp wondered if he was involved with the disappearance of Martin Blevins in 1887.

PINKERTON NATIONAL DETECTIVE AGENCY

In 1890, Horn worked for Horace and Burt Dunlap at the Dunlap Ranch. He met "Doc" Shores, a US deputy marshal, helping him recover stolen horses. Doc also worked part-time for the Pinkerton National Detective Agency. He recommended Horn, who was hired shortly thereafter. Horn liked the status of being a Pinkerton Detective and worked out of the Denver office. He helped catch the train robbers in the Cotopaxi Robbery of August 1891. But as a detective, it became apparent that he was a lone wolf who was willing to shoot first. His investigation of the train wreck not far from Salem, Oregon, didn't pan out. He didn't fit the "uptown" image of a squeaky-clean agency man. Seemingly, he played both sides of the law. He was arrested for robbery in Reno, Nevada, and was forced to resign. A fellow Pinkerton Detective, who worked with him, Charlie Siringo, felt Horn was rather talented but blurred the lines. Siringo later wrote that the head of the Pinkertons, William Pinkerton himself, confided that Horn should have gone to prison for his larceny, but the agency fought the charges to protect its image. Through some maneuvering, the jury acquitted him. The agency breathed a sigh of relief.

THE CATTLE DETECTIVE

Wyoming in 1893 become a perfect storm. The Johnson County War proved a costly mistake for large ranchers. Intimidation, lynching, and murders—never mind hiring a trainload of hired guns from Texas—didn't settle with the public or the courts. A cattle detective was a fraction of the cost and could move with precision. Horn's last job with the Pinkertons, a minor role at the end of the Johnson County War, put him in the right place. He was hired by the Swan Land and Cattle Company to patrol the range and gather evidence so offenders could be tried in court. Playing by the rules posed a problem. Catching rustlers and bringing them to trial was easier than getting convictions. Too many judges and juries favored homesteaders and small ranches. And if they were lucky enough to get a conviction, it was little more than a proverbial slap on the hand. Such tidings soured large ranchers on the system.

The Langhoff Ranch was an example. After a timely investigation in 1893, Horn built his case. To make his evidence airtight in court, he collected Alexander Bowie, one of Swan Ranch managers, and two honorable men who could give firsthand testimony. The year before, 1892, John Clay and John Coble had charged Fred and Eva Langhoff for horse theft. There wasn't enough evidence for a conviction, but Fred feared for his life and left Wyoming. The four rode up to the barn after dark and caught the thieves, literally red-handed. They were butchering Swan beef by lantern light. One of the men started to threaten them with his knife. Horn said, "Drop that knife or I'll put a bullet through your heart." Everyone knew he meant it. Thus, at gunpoint, the thieves were disarmed and taken to town to face the law. Five were charged, including Eva. One of the men was given a prison sentence, eighteen months, but was pardoned early. It's also likely that Horn became acquainted with Coble at this time. Chip Carlson, in *Blood on the Moon*, sums up the cattleman's mood in the words of Thomas Adams, president of the Wyoming Stock Growers Association. Adams wrote, "[we have] been thrown out of court and laughed at for our pains. Circumstances have forced cattlemen to look to themselves for protection."

If the courts were not going to do their part, there was something called "Winchester justice," and they had Tom Horn.

"A SYSTEM THAT NEVER FAILS"

On the morning of July 31, William Lewis was loading stolen meat onto a wagon. He took three bullets in the chest. Each bullet was fatal; so three sent a message. It was a hot summer and unfortunately Lewis's body wasn't found for several days. The smell was foul, and his body bloated and blackened by the hot, dry wind. The inquest was short, and Lewis was buried on the spot. He had been a disagreeable fellow with a long record. Several years previously, he'd been arrested and found guilty of rustling, but somehow, he had been granted a new trial. He won. Next, he committed another unforgivable transgression, Lewis countersued the Swan Cattle Company, Coble, and other important people. He had a chance of winning because a loss might have bankrupted some of those named.

It had been a bloody year, but 1895 was about to get worse.

Seven miles from the Lewis murder, on September 10, 1895, the one-armed Fred Powell took a bullet in the chest. Hired hand Andrew Ross heard the shot and found the body. Earlier, Ross had been charged with grand larceny, as well as cattle and horse rustling. Previously that same year, he'd been sentenced to four months in jail for stealing a horse. The charges were dropped. The *Boomerang*, Laramie's newspaper, on September 10, 1895, wrote that Powell had been warned three times. "Mr. Powell: This is your third and last warning. There are three things for you to do— quit killing other people's cattle or be killed yourself or leave the country . . . at once."

The cattle barons, and Horn himself, considered his action justice and not murder. To add to his mystique as judge-jury-executioner, Horn would receive implied approval from the governor of Wyoming, W. A. Richards. Richards was not only governor, but he was also interested in Horn's work on a personal level because he was also a Wyoming rancher. Charles Penrose wrote about the meeting in his memoir, *The Rustlers Business*. Penrose's friend, W. C. Irvine, who was the head of the Wyoming Stock Growers Association, wrote Penrose about the visit:

> *[The Governor] said he would like to meet Tom Horn, but hesitated to have him come to the Governor's office. I [Irvine] said, 'Stroll in my office . . . at three o'clock this afternoon, and I will have him there."*
> *[At the meeting] the Governor was quite nervous, so was I. Horn perfectly cool. He talked generally, was careful of his ground; he told the Governor he would either drive every rustler out of Big Horn County, or take no pay other than $350 advanced to buy two horses and a pack outfit. When he had finished the job to the Governor's satisfaction, he should receive $5,000, because, he said in conclusion, 'whenever everything else fails, I have a system which never does.' He placed no limit on the number of men to be gotten rid of. This*

almost stunned the Governor. He immediately showed an inclination to shorten the interview. . . . [After Horn left] the Governor said to me, 'So that is Tom Horn! A very different man from what I expected to meet. Why, he is not bad-looking, and is quite intelligent; but a cool devil, ain't he?'

Irvine would say Horn could kill without a thought. Horn appeared to have been a person of interest and that the grand jury voted for indictment, but apparently Coble's intimidating influence was powerful. Nevertheless, Coble thought it advisable that his friend Horn leave the state for a while. *The Rocky Mountain News*, linking Coble and Horn for the first time, was critical of the legal system for not doing its duty.

For the next few years, he moved like a paladin, an enfranchised black knight "enforcer," executing the interests of powerful men. In 1898, he served as a packer for the Fifth Corps and the Rough Riders in the Spanish American War. He was not a combatant but saw action and contracted yellow fever. He was sent home to recover and then convalesced at the Coble ranch. He did some investigation on the famous Wilcox Train Robbery in 1899, attributed to Butch Cassidy and the Wild Bunch. When rancher Ora Ben Haley complained about rustling at a meeting in 1900, Coble knew who to recommend. (See chapter on Brown's Hole.)

Maybe it was an honest moment of reflection, maybe he was bragging, but Horn made an important observation. He couched it by talking about the Apache Wars and how he found a trooper "spread-eagled on an ant hill" or teamsters roped to wagon wheels upside down over small fires "until their brains was exploded right out o' their skulls," or how in Texas he'd heard of cattleman "wrappin' a cow thief up in green hides" so he suffocated in the heat. But he concluded, "one thing I just don't think there is, and that's a sportin' way o' killin' a man."

WILLIE NICKELL IS SHOT

The year 1901 would prove to be a bad one. Horn's reputation had caught up with him. There was always trouble with the smaller ranchers. Horn had been hired to patrol Iron Mountain. To make things interesting, playing out like a soap opera, a nasty feud was boiling between two small ranchers, the Nickells and Millers, and then throw sheep into the equation, adding a decade-long antipathy between John Coble and Kels Nickell. In 1890, Coble, an owner of a large ranch, was trying to get rid of Nickell, a damned homesteader. Nickell confronted Coble at the station. Angry words were exchanged. Fiery Coble began to draw his pistol but fiery Nickell was faster, stabbing his bowie knife deep into Coble's guts. Coble nearly died from the wound. He healed but his anger festered. By 1901, Coble's anger had become explosive. Let's take a careful look at what is sometimes called the Nickell timeline.

On Wednesday, July 17, 1901, Tom left the nearby Miller ranch in the morning. The next day, around 7 a.m. young Willie Nickell was shot nearly a mile from his ranch house. He had ridden his father's horse and dismounted to open the gate. Two bullets tore into his back, exiting through the chest. He ran, stumbled, and fell facedown. His father, Kels Nickell, heard shots after but wasn't concerned; shots were common enough since everyone hunted for the pot. Willie wasn't missed because he was supposed to be spending the night with a neighbor.

When Willie didn't show up on Friday, July 19, Kels Nickell sent his son Freddie to look. Freddie discovered Willie's body and raced back to the ranch yelling, "Willie had been murdered." Willie's body was brought home in a wagon.

There was a coroner's inquest at the Nickell ranch on Saturday, July 20. The public was shocked by the murder of the boy. About one hundred miles away, midmorning, Horn arrived at the Coble ranch. He cleaned up, rode to Laramie ten miles away and went on a ten-day drinking binge with Frank Stone. (He sobered up on July 31.)

On Sunday, July 21, Willie's body was taken to Cheyenne. The coroner's inquest continued, and an autopsy was performed. As early as the first inquest, a working theory was that Kels Nickell was the target. Suspicion falls on the Millers.

Willie was buried in Cheyenne on July 23. Kels suggested the head of the boy was purposefully positioned on a flat rock after he was shot.

About ten days later, on August 4, Kels Nickell was ambushed and shot but recovers.

The sheriff's department was spread thin, so the county asked US deputy marshal Joe LeFors to help with the investigation on August 6.

The inquest continued on August 8, and Victor Miller and his sons were arrested, jailed, and questioned.

The coroner's inquest questions Glendolene Myrtle Kimmel, the schoolteacher, who would later try to help Horn and assist him with his autobiography, on August 9. Horn was also called to testify. He stated he was not in the area at the time and had witnesses to verify it.

JOE LEFORS BUILDS HIS CASE

Joe LeFors came to Wyoming in the 1880s with a herd of Texas cattle. He'd been a cowboy, brand inspector, investigator, and US deputy marshal. He'd also tracked, unsuccessfully, members of the Wild Bunch. There were rumors, of course, about Horn's involvement but that was nothing new. It wasn't until LeFors interviewed George Prentice that he began to suspect Horn. Prentice was the liaison between Frank Bosler, investor, and John Coble, rancher. The Bosler empire was famously vast and successful. It included ranches in Wyoming, among other states, as well as industrial and mining interests. Prentice mentioned to LeFors that the cattle association was frustrated with the negative publicity generated by Horn. Then Prentice told LeFors that he had been the ranch agent who had paid Horn for killing Lewis and Powell in 1895.

LeFors, fully aware that a conviction would launch his career and might open opportunities with the movers and shakers, began to plot Horn's downfall. Aware of his weaknesses, LeFors developed a plan to hook Horn and play him like a trout on a dry fly and then swoop him into his net. Late in December 1901, Horn was at Coble's ranch. When Coble was in Cheyenne, LeFors asked Coble to take a letter to Horn about a business opportunity. Of course the letter was a sham, but it was a key element in the sting. It was about a "possible" cattle detective job in Montana; LeFors explained that his friend, Sheriff W. D. Smith in Miles City, needed "secret work" done and Horn might be the right man, if interested. Sheriff Smith had rustling problems in the Big Moon River area. The pay would be "$125 a month and [Horn could] make good wages besides [implied bonuses for killing rustlers]." Smith, by the way, was a real lawman in Montana who owed LeFors a favor and agreed to the charade.

Horn wrote back expressing his interest, saying "it couldn't be worse than Brown's Hole." The two agreed to meet so LeFors could clear up the details, give Horn a letter of introduction and get him on his way. A gullible Horn gulped at the proverbial dry fly LeFors crafted and presented. Horn knew he had the curriculum vitae for the job, needing only to "talk himself up."

Before he caught the train to Cheyenne on January 11, 1902, Horn started drinking to celebrate his good fortune. The two met in town, but LeFors suggested they go to his office. He had a bottle, and they could discuss the job privately. The trap was set. In another room, Deputy Leslie Snow and stenographer Charles Olnhaus were waiting patiently. The sworn-in lawman could testify about what Horn would say while Stenographer Olnhaus recorded every word. To protect their safety, LeFors had a one-way lock on the door. There was a mattress on the floor, and the bottom of the door had been planed so the two could hear. There were also holes in the door so they could see. Horn might have seen through the ploy if he'd had his wits, but dulled by alcohol and the additional drinks the marshal had plied him with, his aggrandized stories would nail his coffin shut.

LeFors asked questions that encouraged Horn to talk about his qualifications. Occasionally, the marshal, presenting his questions as "one professional to another," would ask why he couldn't find tracks at the Nickell shooting. Horn mentioned something about going barefooted. LeFors would ask another question about picking up the empty shells. Horn said, "You bet your [expletive deleted] life I did." He lead Horn into ninety-proof confessions about shooting Lewis and Powell in 1895. Horn would make so many self-incriminating statements, that even if the stenographer got a few things wrong, LeFors and other lawmen felt his guilt was overwhelming. One famous remark was a highlight in the interview. Tom said, "It was the best shot I ever made and the dirtiest trick I ever done." Other questions were directed at his alleged admission of murdering Willie Nickell using his .30-30 rifle, the placing of a stone under the boy's head, and being paid $2,100.

The stenographer worked all night, transcribed his notes, and had a typed manuscript of the confession to Sheriff Smalley by January 12. Smalley obtained a warrant to arrest Horn for murder. Still on a drinking spree at the Inter-Ocean Hotel, LeFors watched as Sheriff Smalley, Deputy Sheriff Richard Proctor, and Cheyenne Chief of Police Sandy McNeil arrested Tom on January 13. Dimmed by drink, Horn was taken aback when the sheriff disarmed him. He was taken to Laramie County Jail where he would spend the rest of his life.

TRIED FOR MURDER

We know the Tom Horn narrative ends with a rope. We also need to remember that he spent twenty-two months in jail. His trial in 1902 was the biggest event to hit Cheyenne, Wyoming. The *Rocky Mountain News* suggested, and rightly so, that the courtroom was like a "circus." Judge Richard H. Scott, who presided over the case was running for reelection and knew a win would look good. The cattlemen wanted Horn to go away. Many local folks felt Horn was guilty and should be hung.

Horn's trial leaves us with questions, and the debate continues to this day. Did he get due process? What about reasonable doubt? What about circumstantial evidence? Is a drunken confession admissible? Then we need to consider that Dr. Barber wasn't sure if the wounds were made by a .30-30 rifle, and the list goes on. Historians agree his reputation as a killer did little to help his case. Chip Carlson in his well-researched book, *Tom Horn: Blood on the Moon*, thinks Horn probably didn't kill Willie Nickell and concedes that "Tom Horn was railroaded."

Tom's two-week trial began on Friday, October 10, 1902. Parts of Horn's confession collected by LeFors were introduced as evidence by Walter Stoll, prosecuting attorney. Were some statements taken out of context? LeFors testified. Horn was placed in the general vicinity, but Otto Plaga testified Horn was twenty miles from the scene of the murder an hour after it was committed. Victor Miller also testified that he also had a .30-30 and that both he and Horn used the same kind of ammunition. Most alarming was the defense letting Horn self-destruct on the stand. The clever prosecuting attorney, Walter Stoll, knew what buttons to push. He prodded Horn into tangents that destroyed his case. Not seeing the setup, Horn took the bait. He further admitted:

> Stoll: At that time . . . were you in a condition to remember whether you had these conversations with these men or not?
> Horn: I remember everything that occurred to me in my life.
> Stoll: You have never been so much under the influence of liquor as to not remember what you said?
> Horn: Not if I could talk.

Two weeks later, the jury returned a guilty verdict on Friday, October 24. Almost a year later, on October 3, 1903, the State Supreme Court upheld the lower court's decision after the process of appeals wound its way through the system.

After he was hung, Horn was buried in the Columbia Cemetery in Boulder, Colorado, on December 3. And, of course, there is a Tom Horn ghost, but that's another story.

JOHN COBLE'S SUICIDE

I've often felt this ended too soon. What about player John Coble? He was said to be lovable and genteel but hot-tempered. He was a college graduate from the East who went to "cowboy in Wyoming." Like Horn, he had his own honor code. He stood by Horn when the Wyoming Stock Growers Association would not. It would almost be touching if we weren't talking about a murder and the guy who hired the murderer. Coble also embezzled at least $5,000 (or more) from his partner/investor, Frank Bosler; these misappropriated funds were earmarked for cattle purchases. He could have spent $10,000 for Horn's defense, but he also paid for a lavish funeral and headstone. The next year he underwrote the publication of the Horn autobiography. Bosler and Coble would soon part ways, fight a difficult lawsuit, and later Coble would lose his ranch. Bosler refused to deal with him again. Coble had bet on Horn and lost. It's speculation, but there was "supposed" to be a lost letter saying that Coble, himself, shot Willie Nickell.

Coble drifted around the West but couldn't catch a break. By 1914, he was desperate. In Elko, Nevada, the *Elko Independent* reported, a despondent Coble asked for stationery at the front desk of the Commercial Hotel. Here are a few lines from his letter, "Believe me, I have tried to pull through. I am IN, I AM ALL IN. Believe me . . . I cannot make good." He went into the ladies' restroom, drew his .32-caliber pistol and blew out his brains.

18

JESSE WASHINGTON

CONVICTED OF MURDER AND LYNCHED IN THE TOWN SQUARE

It's a very ugly part of history. I regret that it happened, but as far as me coming out to apologize. . . . I didn't have anything to do with it.
—Ray Meadows, Waco County commissioner

WACO, TEXAS, 1916

On Monday, May 8, 1916, fifty-three-year-old Lucy Fryer was violently murdered on her farm; her body was found near the door of a "sod shed." A doctor confirmed that she was deceased prior to "allegedly" being sexually assaulted. She left behind a husband, George, and children between the ages of fifteen to twenty-two.

The prime suspect in the murder was Jesse Washington, an intellectually disabled Black teenager who had worked at the Fryer farm for five months. During the questioning he admitted to the murder. Presumably law enforcement told him that if he "confessed to the killing, the officers would keep him from being lynched by vigilantes." Because he was illiterate, Washington marked his *X* at the bottom of his confession, and the next day it was printed in all the papers. Washington had told the officers where he'd hidden the hammer he'd used to kill his employer. Because he'd been plowing a field, he had hidden the hammer in the brush at the end of a furrow. When found, the hammer had blood and a scattering of cotton seeds on it.

After he was arrested, Sheriff Samuel S. Fleming took Washington to a neighboring county to be questioned. As news of the murder spread, there was talk of a lynching. Vigilantes arrived with a rope only to discover Washington's absence; he'd been relocated. The newspaper praised the vigilantes' efforts to seek justice.

"JUST PRAY, JESSE!"

To indict Washington, a special session of the grand jury was held on May 11, 1916. His defense counselor was able to consult with him prior to the beginning of the trial. The defense's advice was just two words, "to pray." Apparently, Washington didn't have a prayer anyway. The Black population in the area was a mere 20 percent, and this lynching would not be the first. A Black man had been lynched at a city bridge in 1905.

Trial by jury is not a figure of speech, but in Washington's case it took the jury exactly "four minutes" to render a verdict of guilty. Washington, a seventeen-year-old farm hand, had used a hammer to bash in Lucy Fryer's skull. His conviction was no surprise, neither was the jury foreman's "sentence of death." This was the ultimate example of a speedy trial.

Washington was mentally incompetent and had no real grasp of what was happening. Officers appeared to escort him back to his cell. He had already pled guilty and had been asked to sign a paper that waived the customary thirty-day period before execution of the sentence. Just outside, an enraged crowd began to push in; they aimed to seize the Black teen and give him exactly what he deserved. The sheriff and other law enforcement had asked the crowd to allow justice to take its course, and they had—sort of. When Washington was first arrested vigilantes arrived to hang him, but they left disappointed because he wasn't in his cell.

After Washington's conviction, vigilantes stormed the courthouse and put him in chains—the shackled collar and leg restraints were reminiscent of a Black man on an auction block or the ironware worn by a coffle of those who were enslaved. He was dragged through the streets; at the outset, he'd tried to fight back. He hit. He punched. He even bit

Lynching at Waco city hall, photograph taken by Fred Gildersleeve on May 15, 1916. COURTESY OF LIBRARY OF CONGRESS/PUBLISHED BY THE NAACP AFTER THEIR INVESTIGATION OF THE LYNCHING IN *THE CRISIS* VOL. 12, SUPPLEMENT TO NO. 3: *THE WACO HORROR*.

someone. This succeeded in riling up the crowd more who took pleasure in poking and prodding him. He was a criminal after all; he should be treated as one.

A large bonfire was lit in the city square near a convenient telephone pole. Washington was bloody and the crowd cheered but things had barely begun. He was held down and castrated; his genitalia became someone's keepsake. A chain was fastened to the chain around his neck and Washington was hoisted above the blaze of the bonfire. Then, slowly he was lowered. Washington shrieked and screamed as his flesh burned, and as if someone heard or cared, he was lifted back up. Inconceivably, he was raised to extend his agony; the crowd didn't want him to burn too quickly. During one frenzied moment Washington tried to escape the fire by pulling himself up the chain. Those closest to the lynching reported he was unable to pull himself up; his fingers had all been severed.

A photograph of the lynching of Jesse Washington in progress. Taken by Fred Gildersleeve on May 15, 1916. COURTESY OF LIBRARY OF CONGRESS/PUBLISHED BY THE NAACP AFTER THEIR INVESTIGATION OF THE LYNCHING IN *THE CRISIS* VOL. 12, SUPPLEMENT TO NO. 3: *THE WACO HORROR.*

"LAWLESS DEMONSTRATION"—A POLITE TERM FOR LYNCHING

A Waco, Texas, newspaper reported the lynching as one of the most "exciting occurrences" in recent history. According to other papers there were "10,000 to 15,000" people watching the event and cheering the activities. This number seems high, but we are certain it was well attended. Because it happened at the noon hour, we're told that schoolchildren were escorted by their teacher to view this turn-of-the-century civics lesson. We're also told that some of the boys climbed nearby trees to get a better glimpse of the body. The schoolchildren were capable of seeing the chief of police, Guy McNamera, and the Waco mayor, John Dallas, in the crowd. They may have overheard county sheriff Fleming "reminding" his officers to stay out of the way and not interfere.

Remains of Jesse Washington's burned body and cinders after lynching in Waco, Texas. ABSTRACT/MEDIUM: 1 PHOTOGRAPHIC PRINT (POSTCARD). COURTESY OF LIBRARY OF CONGRESS

Sooner or later the majority could get a good view. They had plenty of time as the process went on for almost two hours; raising and then lowering Washington again and again into the fire. They didn't want him to die too quickly. Some read in the paper and some heard it at the trial: Washington was asked if he was guilty, and he had flatly stated, "That's what I done."

With all the lifting up and lowering Washington was mostly burned by the time the endless two hours concluded. But, for those who really wanted a souvenir to remember the day, you could reportedly purchase one of his teeth.

19

TEXAS RANGERS

SOMETIMES AN INSTRUMENT OF ETHNIC CLEANSING

Ranger Captain Bill McDonald arrived in Langtry, Texas, to stop a fight. The mayor asked where the rest of the rangers were. McDonald supposedly said, "Hell, ain't I enough?"

PORVENIR, TEXAS, 1918

It happened early in the morning of January 24, 1918. Texas Rangers and soldiers rode into Porvenir, a sleepy Latino village of goat herders in the Big Bend Region near the Mexican border. A month earlier on Christmas Day, Mexican revolutionaries had raided, robbed, and killed at the Brite Ranch, forty miles away. The men searched the village looking for property that might be cached. While searching the shacks, a ranger discovered a pair of boots resembling a pair that had been reported stolen; another ranger found two firearms. The men didn't have a search warrant or probable cause, and the evidence they found was questionable. What herder in a white or Mexican village didn't have a few guns for coyotes, wolves, or mountain lions? In the moonlight, the lawmen rounded up fifteen sleepy men and boys, ages sixteen to seventy, and marched them to a nearby bluff. Maybe it was a vendetta attack. Maybe it was retaliation for Brite Ranch. At first it was rumored revolutionaries were hiding in the village or the townspeople had been involved. Before the sun rose there were widows and forty-two orphans. Most villagers fled across the Rio Grande to Mexico. Legend has it that the next morning an old woman driving a horse cart arrived to retrieve the bodies. Officials razed and burned the village; it had been home to 142 people.

At first it was called a "shoot-out." Later, the State Department said that a Texas Ranger had been involved in the killing. In June 1918, the governor fired several leaders of the Texas Rangers and relocated others. A State of Texas investigation concluded that the Rangers were guilty of "gross violations" of the law, but no one was charged. It's easy to place blame for Porvenir on acts of racial intolerance. But that's not entirely fair because the Texas Rangers were state police; more correctly, they often functioned as surgical instruments of politicians rooted in Southern tradition. The issue-driven and outcome-based Texas Rangers frequently took the law into their own hands to achieve assigned objectives. This was expected and winked at. "A Ranger," according to Ranger Captain Bob Crowder, "is an officer who is able to handle any given situation without definite instructions from his commanding officer or higher authority." The massacre at Porvenir was not isolated, nor was it the last.

It was a troubled, dangerous time on the Texas border. The Mexican Revolution lasted ten years. In 1916 Francisco "Pancho" Villa with 1,500 men had attacked Columbus, New Mexico, where nineteen Americans were killed. The Mexican Revolution was bloody and had driven many Mexican citizens to escape to the United States. Before it was concluded, a million Mexicans would lose their lives. American ranchers and farmers on the border lived in fear. Mexican revolutionary forces and bandits had terrorized the West Texas border. In Presidio County, Mexican raids had hit Boquillas, Glen Springs, and the Brite Ranch. The residents in the Big Bend area were ready to strike back. By 1915, the tension on the border was untenable, and something had to be done. The Texas governor, James Ferguson, sent Texas Rangers to get the job done. More than three hundred suspects were shot or lynched without due process.

A company of the Texas Rangers' frontier battalion, circa 1885.
WIKIPEDIA, PUBLIC DOMAIN.

Although the Texas Rangers sometimes wore good guy "white hats" and did remarkable things to protect and serve, portions of their story isn't pleasing. They have hands bloodied by racial violence. If you were to ask a white Texan about the Rangers in the nineteenth century, you'd get a much different answer than the same question posed to someone of Mexican, African, or Indigenous heritage. From the early days of the republic until the Civil War, one of their duties was hunting runaway slaves—often crossing state or international borders. They had their share of stand-up fights with American Indians and Mexicans in the Texas Revolution and the War with Mexico, and sometimes they blurred the lines. One of their de facto duties, especially during Reconstruction, was to enforce Jim Crow and Juan Crow policies. For example, in 1877 when a group of Buffalo Soldiers (Black soldiers) flirted with Mexican ladies, the Texas Rangers felt they needed to correct such egregious behavior. It ended with guns being fired. The Rangers were sometimes referred to as the KKK of the Texas border.

HOW WE LOOK AT THE TEXAS RANGERS

The myth driving this legend is so good and so pleasing, we desperately want it to be true. In fact, we hope it is true. After all, everything is bigger in the Lone Star State. It seems unpatriotic to say otherwise. Who wants to meddle with the sacred? The Texas Ranger represents an ideal Western ethos, and, yes, an ideal Texas ethos. Often a lone ranger, he is tough and so incorruptible he can't be bought. He's intrepid enough to stand up to a town of outlaws or take on a party of Comanche Indians with his saddle rifle and six-guns. It was said that to be a ranger you must "ride like a Mexican, track like a Comanche, and fight like the devil." In song and story, the Texas Rangers were larger than life, all but reaching the status of mythic superheroes. In legend and lore, they often rode alone because, essentially, it took only one Ranger to clean up a town gone bad, and a single ranger could face a dozen outlaws without blinking. These lawmen fought Indians and kept the peace for the decent farmers, ranchers, and town folk. They brought in outlaws, dead or alive, returned stolen cattle, and were not above rescuing a kitten for a little girl in a gingham dress. While the bravery of some Texas Rangers can't be questioned, they were not bulletproof, and like the Royal Canadian Mounted Police, the rangers *somehow* fostered the best public relations of any law enforcement group in the West. The shadow of the Canadian Mounties and the Rangers looms larger than fact. They didn't always do it equitably—especially if you weren't white . . . or if you were organizing a labor union. Although this group of lawmen kept the peace, it was more often a *white* peace. One of the duties of the Texas Rangers was to protect frontier settlements, and this meant making raids and killing as many Indians as they could. During a famous double cross, Rangers helped soldiers kill thirty-five Comanche Indian women and children, including the men who wanted to broker peace. As noted, the Rangers as slave hunters were legendary. In 1838, the Rangers were involved in a battle with an armed group of escaped slaves. One man they worked over with their bowie knives, and the others were sold back into slavery. They each pocketed part of the $800 sale.

THE MYTH AND THE REAL STORY

There is a line between fact and fiction, but sometimes the line is woolly. Does historical fact take the fun out of Old West stories? I certainly hope not. Sometimes it's disappointing to learn our heroes weren't true heroes. There is a famous line in one of the truly great Westerns that addresses this. In *The Man Who Shot Liberty Valance*, Maxwell Scott declares, "When the legend becomes fact, print the legend." Sometimes it happens accidentally or by chance, and other times it's manufactured. This poses a challenge: How do we to view our history? We love the adventure and "romance" of the West; it's a celebration of our heritage. Conceivably it's beneficial to study the West the way we view Greek mythology and Greek history. *The Iliad* and *The Odyssey* are among my favorite pieces of literature. I learned about the myths when I was a child. Knowing the literature and the mythology of the Greeks never dampened my appreciation of the Greek history. I'm a Western fiction and movie buff, but I don't have to deconstruct my favorite films or books. I get caught up in stories of the Old West and enjoy them immensely. Fiction based on truth, not truth based on fiction.

The problem occurs when we realign the truth to fit the fictional narrative or when we pass off—carelessly or inadvertently—the narrative as truth. Heroes and stories are important, especially heroes based on real characters. We want heroes; we need heroes. But if we create demigods carelessly and give them a heroes' breath of life, when their verisimilitude crumbles, when facts prove they have feet of clay, we shouldn't grieve? In this day of connectivity, it takes only a few clicks to find the real story, but the truth should not be a crisis of historical faith. Look at it as adding another texture; it's like adding depth or color to something that was monochrome and two-dimensional.

HISTORIC OVERVIEW OF THE TEXAS RANGERS

We tend to think of the Rangers as a highly trained, cohesive unit of state police. Certainly, they were stretched thin—eleven European countries can fit inside Texas. A place to start is looking at the Texas Rangers before and after 1874. As the historian Robert Utley suggests in *Lone Star Justice*, before 1874, the Rangers were "citizen soldiers intermittently mobilized

Texas Rangers' current badge and Mexican coin.
HARTMANN352, PUBLIC DOMAIN, VIA WIKIMEDIA COMMONS.

for temporary duty to fight Indians or Mexicans." Utley correctly assumes that a better comparison, "regardless of formal designation" would be more like "mounted volunteers, riflemen, minute men." Their job was not primarily law enforcement, although they chased outlaws, but safeguarding the settlements and taking offensive measures against both American Indian and Mexican threats. After 1874, the Texas legislature funded the Rangers, "for the protection of the frontier state of Texas," making them a full-time force.

During their tenure, the Texas Rangers served under the direction of the Texas colony of Mexico, the Republic of Texas, the US army, and the State of Texas. In 1823, Stephen F. Austin realized he needed a way to way to protect his colonies from Comanche Indian raids; he hired ten men to "range" around for the "common defense." These men, called "rangers," were volunteers who were paid $15 a month, and when it was peaceful, they went home and worked their farms. In 1835, a Ranger unit was created to keep the frontier safe. This was more like a full-time job, but they voted for their own leaders. There were fifty-six men in three companies headed by a captain. A major was over the companies. Officers were paid the same wage as the dragoons. They brought their own weapons and arms and had to have enough powder and balls for one hundred shots. During the Texas Revolution, they fought Mexicans, but their main job was to patrol the frontier and keep settlements safe. By 1837 after the Texas Revolution, Captain John Coffee "Jack" Hayes, a hero, was made captain. Their numbers were few; the Comanche attacks were especially problematic. The new Republic ordered almost two hundred .36-caliber Patterson Colts, and these newfangled revolvers were a game changer. Instead of single shots, each revolver would fire five times. A Ranger armed with two Colt revolvers was a force to be reckoned with. This kind of firepower changed the outcome of many battles with the Comanche Indians. However, the Patterson could be temperamental because the trigger was supposed to dropped when the hammer was cocked, and it sometime stuck. But even with trigger issues, the weapon offered substantial firepower. With the success of the Patterson Colt, Samuel Colt and Texas Ranger, Samuel Walker, collaborated. The result was the new Walker Colt. This new weapon, produced in 1847, was a marked improvement in frontier firepower. The Walker Colt was a six-shot in .44 caliber and had a trigger guard and fixed trigger.

During the War with Mexico, 1846–1848, the Rangers were fierce fighters, serving as trackers and guerilla fighters. In 1859 when Juan Nepomuceno Cortina decided to claim Brownsville as well as the land below the Nueces River for Mexico, Texas sent a company of rangers captained by a man nicknamed "Rest in Peace," John S. "Rip" Ford. It was a costly fight. Purportedly Cortina lost 151 men, but it was costly for the

Violence against Latinos Was Rarely Punished

A teenage boy was apparently sitting too close to the door of a saloon while he whittled on a stick. After having a few drinks, a group of men were feeling pretty tough. As they came out the door, they started abusing the fourteen-year-old. It was impertinent for a Mexican to sit so close to the door; the proprietor came and threw him in the street for good measure. This was good fun, so a few more men joined the baiting. As the bullying continued, the boy began to panic. Suddenly, he felt threatened as the men got rougher. He defended himself with his knife. In the scuffle, he stabbed a man who was especially bold. The wound proved fatal. It was Thorndale, Texas, after all, so the men decided to save the town the expense of sending this kid through the legal system. They'd teach him; a Mexican had killed a white man. They fastened a chain around his neck and paraded the boy about town before they hung him.

Time and again history is written by winners, and until recently, we didn't hear much about the *other* groups of people who lived in the Lone Star State. As one historian said, "We can't go back and change what happened, but we can try and tell it right, including the stories that seem to have been forgotten or swept under the rug." The truth is thousands of Latinos were victims of racial violence in Texas; there was little recourse. In the early days, some excellent land was owned by a number of Mexican families. The new settlers speculated the Mexicans might be helping runaway slaves slip across the Rio Grande—or worse—they might want to unite with Black people and incite a rebellion that would dislodge the "rightful" owners off their newly acquired land. In a panic, several Texas counties forced Mexican landowners to leave. Near Austin, Mexicans were not allowed to stay unless a respectable white vouched for them. In northern Texas, Refugio Ramirez, his wife, and teenage daughter were killed for "bewitching" folks in Collin, Texas. After a twenty-year-old migrant worker was manhandled out his jail cell in Rocksprings, Texas, a mob tied him to a tree and set him ablaze.

Texans, too. Around eighty Texans and Rangers were killed in the battle. The Mexican soldiers nicknamed the fighters "Los Diablos Tejanos," the Texas Devils. During the Civil War, many Rangers joined the Confederate Army. To protect Texas borders and settlements, the Rangers enlisted young boys, old men, and those who could serve in the army. In 1874 Captain Leander McNelly organized a group of Rangers in DeWitt County, often called the Frontier Battalion. They participated in fifteen battles along with the US Cavalry with the Indians. By 1875 the Comanches and Kiowa nations were all but defeated, so Captain McNelly and the Rangers tackled the "Lawless Nueces Strip," a wild piece of real estate from Corpus Christi to the Rio Grande. During the "Las Cueras War," the Rangers, violating international law, crossed the Rio Grande, attacked Mexican nationals, and brought back stolen cattle.

BIBLIOGRAPHY

Abbott, Edith. *Women in Industry: A Study in American Economic History*. New York: D. Appleton and Co., 1910.

Ahmad, Diana. *The Opium Debate and Chinese Exclusion Laws in the Nineteenth-Century American West*. Reno: University of Nevada Press, 2011.

Aldridge, Dorothy. *Historic Colorado City: The Town with a Future*. Colorado Springs, CO: Little London Press, 1996.

Anderson, Gary Clayton. *The Conquest of Texas: Ethnic Cleansing in the Promised Land, 1820–1875*. Norman: University of Oklahoma Press, 2019.

Armitage, Susan, and Elizabeth Jameson, eds. *The Women's West*. Norman: University of Oklahoma Press, 1987.

Barnhart, Jacqueline Baker. *The Fair but Frail: Prostitution in San Francisco, 1849–1900*. Reno: University of Nevada Press, 1986.

Barra, Allen. *Inventing Wyatt Earp: His Life and Many Legends*. Lincoln: University of Nebraska Press, 2009.

Barry, Theodore Augustus, and B. A. Patten. *Men and Memories of San Francisco in the Spring of '50*. San Francisco, CA: A. L. Bancroft and Company, 1873.

Billington, Ray Allen. *America's Frontier Heritage*. New York: Holt, Rinehart and Winston, 1966.

Blair, Edward, and E. Richard Churchill. *Everybody Came to Leadville*. Leadville, CO: Timberline Books, 1971.

Brooks, Juanita. *The Mountain Meadows Massacre*. Norman: University of Oklahoma Press, 1999.

Brown, Dee, Martin F. Schmitt, and Martin F. Schmitt. *The American West*. London: Pocket, 2004.

Burroughs, John Rolfe. *Where the Old West Stayed Young*. New York: Bonanza Books, 1962.

Butler, Anne M., and Ona Siporin. *Uncommon Common Women: Ordinary Lives of the West*. Logan: Utah State University Press, 1996.

Carrigan, William D., and Clive Webb. *Forgotten Dead: Mob Violence against Mexicans in the United States, 1848–1928*. Oxford: Oxford University Press, 2013.

Chidsey, Donald Barr. *The California Gold Rush*. New York: Crown, 1968.

DeJournette, Dick, and Daun DeJournette. *One Hundred Years of Brown's Park and Diamond Mountain*. Vernal, UT: DeJournette Enterprises, 1997.

DeVoto, Bernard. *Across the Wide Missouri*. Boston: Houghton Mifflin, 1998.

Diaz, George T. *Border Contraband: A History of Smuggling across the Rio Grande*. Austin: University of Texas Press, 2015.

DiLorenzo, Thomas J. "The Culture of Violence in the American West: Myth versus Reality." *Independent Review* 15, no. 2 (2010): 227–40.

Dimsdale, Thomas J. *The Vigilantes of Montana*. Norman: University of Oklahoma Press, 1953.

Dodds, Joanne West. *What's a Nice Girl Like You Doing in a Place like This? Prostitution in Southern Colorado 1860 to 1911*. Pueblo, CO: Focal Plain, 1996.

Dykes, J. C. *Billy the Kid: The Biography of a Legend*. Albuquerque: University of New Mexico Press, 1952.

Dykstra, Robert R. *The Cattle Towns*. Lincoln: University of Nebraska Press, 1983.

Finnegan, Frances. *Poverty and Prostitution: A Study of Victorian Prostitutes in York*. Cambridge: Cambridge University Press, 1979.

Gillett, James B. *Six Years with the Texas Rangers 1875 to 1881*. Lincoln: University of Nebraska Press, 1976.

Hine, Robert V., and John Mack Faragher. *Frontiers: A Short History of the American West*. New Haven, CT: Yale University Press, 2008.

———. *The American West: An Interpretive History*. New Haven CT: Yale University Press, 2000.

Horn, Tom. *Life of Tom Horn: Government Scout & Interpreter, Written by Himself*. Denver, CO: Louthan Book Company, 1904. (Reprint Norman: University of Oklahoma Press, 1964.)

Hunter, J. Marvin. *The Trail Drivers of Texas*. Austin: University of Texas Press, 1996.

Jeffrey, Julie Roy. *Frontier Women: "Civilizing" the West? 1840–1880*. New York: Hill and Wang, 1999.

Jensen, Joan M., and Darlis A. Miller. "The Gentle Tamers Revisited: New Approaches to the History of Women in the American West." *Pacific Historical Review* 49, no. 2 (May 1, 1980): 173–213. https://doi.org/10.2307/3638899.

Johnson, Susan Lee. *Roaring Camp: The Social World of the California Gold Rush*. New York: W. W. Norton, 2001.

Kessler-Harris, Alice. *Out to Work: A History of Wage-Earning Women in the United States*. Oxford: Oxford University Press, 2003.

The Man Who Shot Liberty Valance. John Ford, director. Paramount, 1962.

McLaughlin, Marie L. *Myths and Legends of the Sioux.* Lincoln: University of Nebraska Press, 1990.

McLoughlin, Denis. *Wild and Woolly: An Encyclopedia of the Old West.* New York: Barnes & Noble Books, 1996.

Miller, Stuart Creighton. *The Unwelcome Immigrant: The American Image of the Chinese, 1785–1882.* Berkeley: University of California Press, 1974.

Morn, Frank. *"The Eye That Never Sleeps": A History of the Pinkerton National Detective Agency.* Bloomington: Indiana University Press, 1982.

Myers, John Myers. *Doc Holliday.* Lincoln: University of Nebraska Press, 1973.

O'Neal, Bill. *Encyclopedia of Western Gunfighters.* Norman: University of Oklahoma Press, 1991.

———. *War in East Texas: Regulators vs. Moderators.* Denton, TX: University of North Texas Press, 2018.

Reieter, Joan Swallow. *The Old West: The Women.* Alexandria, VA: Time-Life Books, 1978.

Rodgers, Daniel T. *Atlantic Crossings: Social Politics in a Progressive Age.* New York: ACLS History E-Book Project, 2004.

Rosa, Joseph G. *The Gunfighter: Man or Myth?* Norman: University of Oklahoma Press, 1989.

Royce, Josiah. *California from the Conquest in 1846 to the Second Vigilance Committee in San Francisco.* New York: Alfred A. Knopf, 1948.

Rutter, Michael. *Bedside Book of Bad Girls: Outlaw Women of the American West.* Helena, MT: Farcountry Press, 2008.

———. *Boudoirs to Brothels: The Intimate World of Wild West Women.* Helena, MT: Farcountry Incorporated, 2015.

———. *Myths and Mysteries of the Old West.* Guilford, CT: TwoDot, 2017.

———. *Outlaw Tales of Utah: True Stories of the Beehive State's Most Infamous Crooks, Culprits, and Cutthroats.* Guilford, CT: TwoDot, 2011.

———. *Upstairs Girls: Prostitution in the American West.* Helena, MT: Farcountry Incorporated, 2012.

———. *Wild Bunch Women.* Guilford, CT: TwoDot, 2003.

Sandoz, Mari. *The Battle of Little Bighorn.* Lincoln: University of Nebraska, 1978.

Scharnhorst, Gary. *Bret Harte: Opening the American Literary West.* Norman: University of Oklahoma Press, 2016.

Shannon, William Vincent. *American Irish.* New York: Macmillan, 1966.

Smith, Joseph. *The Joseph Smith Papers, Journals*. Edited by Dean C. Jessee, Ronald K. Esplin, Richard Lyman Bushman, Mark Ashurst-McGee, and Richard L. Jensen. Salt Lake City, UT: Church Historian's Press, 2008.

Sonnichsen, C. L. *Ten Texas Feuds*. Albuquerque: University of New Mexico Press, 2000.

Stevens, J. David. "'She War a Woman': Family Roles, Gender, and Sexuality in Bret Harte's Western Fiction." *American Literature* 69, no. 3 (1997): 571. https://doi.org/10.2307/2928215.

Swanson, Doug J. *Cult of Glory: The Bold and Brutal History of the Texas Rangers*. New York: Penguin Books, 2021.

Turner, Frederick Jackson. *The Significance of the Frontier in American History*. Mansfield Centre, CT: Martino Publishing, 2014.

Twain, Mark. *Roughing It*. New York: Harper & Brothers, 1899.

Utley, Robert M. *Billy the Kid: A Short and Violent Life*. Lincoln: University of Nebraska Press, 1989.

———. *The Lance and the Shield: The Life and Times of Sitting Bull*. New York: Ballantine Books, 1993.

Walker, Ronald W., Richard E. Turley, and Glen M. Leonard. *Massacre at Mountain Meadows*. Oxford: Oxford University Press, 2011.

Warner, Matt, and Murray E. King. *The Last of the Bandit Raiders*. New York: Bonanza, 1960.

White, Richard. *It's Your Misfortune and None of My Own: A New History of the American West*. Norman: University of Oklahoma Press, 1993.

Wilson, John P. *Merchants, Guns, & Money: The Story of Lincoln County and Its Wars*. Santa Fe, NM: Museum of New Mexico Press, 1987.

Woodworth, Jed, and Richard L. Bushman. *Joseph Smith: Rough Stone Rolling*. New York: Alfred A. Knopf, 2005.

Worster, Donald. "Beyond the Agrarian Myth." Edited by Patricia Nelson Limerick, Clyde A Milner II, and Charles E Rankin. *Trails: Toward a New Western History*, n.d., 3–25. https://doi.org/10.2307/j.ctt22h6q2f.4.

Wright, Robert Marr. *Dodge City, the Cowboy Capital: And the Great Southwest in the Days of the Wild Indian, the Buffalo, the Cowboy, Dance Halls, Gambling Halls and Bad Men*. Wichita, Kansas: Wichita Eagle Press, 1913.

Yung, Judy, Gordon H. Chang, and H. Mark Lai. *Chinese American Voices: From the Gold Rush to the Present*. Berkeley: University of California Press 2012.

INDEX

ABOUT THE AUTHOR

Michael Rutter is a writer/photographer who has published fifty books and hundreds of articles for magazines, journals, and newspapers. He is a recipient of the Ben Franklin Book Award for Excellence and the Rocky Mountain Book Publishers' Award. An "addicted" fly fisherman, his outdoor essays have been widely published (from Yale University to *Outdoor Life*). Michael has worked with American Experience on "The Wild West Series" and is interviewed in the A&E documentary *Butch Cassidy and the Sundance Kid* (Netflix, PBS). He has been a Christa McAuliffe Fellow and an AT&T Scholar. He has worked in advertising and as a consultant. He has been a key contractor with Qualtrics, specializing in executive communications and management training.

His books include *Colorado Madams*; *Utah off the Beaten Path*; *Myths and Mysteries of the Old West*, *Boudoirs to Brothels: The Intimate World of Wild West Women*; *Wild Bunch Women*; *Upstairs Girls: Prostitution in the American West*; *Outlaw Tales of Utah*; *Bedside Book of Bad Girls: Outlaw Women of the American West*; *Fly Fishing Made Easy*; and *Basic Essentials Fly Fishing*. Michael has also cowritten textbooks on business, marketing, and technical communication.

Michael and his wife, Shari, spend their summers wandering, photographing bears and other wildlife, digging into historical documents, and throwing copious amounts of fly line. He teaches advanced writing at Brigham Young University and lives in Orem, Utah, with Shari, two cats, and a large, spoiled dog, a Turkish Akbash named Star.